MEMORI
NEWTOWN _____
and BRADGATE HOUSE
edited by Joan Stevenson

THE RESEARCHERS
Joan Stevenson, Lucile Thompson and Janet Neaverson

THE CORE GROUP (who met regularly for over a year)
Kitty Brown, born 1906
Florrie Anderson (née Harrison), born 1911
Evelyn Allsop (née Callis), now of Anstey, born 1914
Mary Woodier (née Matts), now of Glenfield, born 1920
Gwen Wakefield (née Jackson), born 1928
(In order to clarify their relationship to village families, the married women above are normally referred to in the text by their maiden names.)

Other Sources of Information and Photographs

A J Harrison, now of Thurcaston
Horace and Lil Brewin
Dinah Henstock of Groby
Maitland Hull of Field Head
Annie Lloyd of Anstey
Rev M J Logan
Wilf and Mary Buthaway
Millicent Johnson

John Richardson
Ann Gimson (née Hurst)
Viv Brown (née Tomlin)
Jenny Whitehead
Christine Smeeton (née Morris)
Margaret Trewin (née Tomlinson)
Brian Anderson
Newtown Linford C.P. School

Pictures on pages 54, 58, 62 courtesy of the Leicester Mercury.

Kairos Press
Newtown Linford
Leicestershire
1994

Copyright © Joan Stevenson 1994
ISBN 1 871344 04 2
First edition

Design and Layout by Robin Stevenson, Kairos Press.
Body text in Century Expanded 10.5 on 12 point.
Imagesetting by CDS Typeset, Leicester.
Reprographics by Midland Precision Studios, Leicester.
Printed in Great Britain by Norwood Press, Anstey, Leicester.

British Library Cataloguing in Publication Data. A catalogue record for
this book is available from the British Library.

Kairos Press
552 Bradgate Road, Newtown Linford, Leicestershire, LE6 0HB

Contents

VILLAGE LIFE IN THE EARLY TWENTIETH CENTURY

Newtown Linford was always a long, strung-out village. Before the modern developments there were twenty-nine houses on the south side of the street and thirty-one on the north side. As everyone lived on Main Street, locations were usually described according to whether they were bottom end (nearest Leicester) or top end. According to the memories of longstanding residents it was a lovely village: everyone was happy and kind, nobody would dream of locking their doors, and everyone helped everyone else as a matter of course.

The old houses are all either timber-framed (often infilled with brick obtained, honestly or otherwise, from the ruins of the house in Bradgate Park) or made of local stone. The roofs are covered in either thatch or local slate (some slate roofs having replaced burnt-down thatched ones).

As in many villages with relatively few surnames because of intermarriage, boys in particular soon gained nicknames. Some names were passed down from father to son over three or four generations.

A J Harrison, son of Butcher Ike, was born in 1902 and recalls that when he was a boy not everyone in the village could read, for school attendance had only become compulsory in 1880. There was neither Post Office nor telephone in the village in those days. Telegrams were brought over from Groby on the postman's ordinary rounds, unless they were deemed urgent, in which case a Groby lad would be asked to cycle over specially after school.

The postman, George Spencer of Groby, walked his round of Newtown and the Forest. Every Saturday morning he brought in four copies of the Leicester Advertiser and delivered them to the Vicar, Rev Bradyll Johnson D.D; Mr Garratt the agent to the Bradgate Estate; Mr Harry Beck at the Bradgate Arms; and to James Crooks of Lane End Farm. When they had been

Nicknames

Harrisons:
Zaddy (Isaac)
Boykin (Florrie's father, George)
Wrinkles (Walter)
Polo (Florrie's Uncle Joe)
Polly Currants, their sister
Butcher Ike (A J's father)
An unrelated Harrison
Bendy (he had a bent knee)
Brewins:
Chip (Horace)
Butcher (Ernie)
Feather (George)
Jackson: Fairy (Gwen's father, Bill)

Mrs Emily Jane Harrison in front of 124 Main Street

read, the papers were passed round the village and the Forest during the week.

Floods were a periodic problem. Several times a year, when the stream came up, the water was a foot deep between the park gates and the Estate Office (now Linford House). On the other hand, ditches were kept open by the numerous farmworkers, so there were few problems with surface water running off the hillside.

A J's paternal grandfather, William Harrison, was head forester to the Bradgate Estate. His maternal grandfather, James Crooks of Lane End Farm, had six teams of fine horses and carted oak timber which William Harrison had felled, mostly from Martinshaw Wood at Ratby. This was taken to Abbey Lane sidings in Leicester, or to Rothley and Quorn sidings, to be used as sleepers for the new Great Central railway in the 1890s.

Florrie Harrison (later Anderson) was born in 1911 in Lilac Cottage, at the 'top end'. Its accommodation was fairly humble, just one room upstairs, and another room plus kitchen downstairs. When she was five, the family moved across the road to a larger cottage, two up/two down, with stone walls and a thatched roof. One thing which pleased them all was that it was a very warm house, due to the thickness of the walls.

A BRANCH OF THE HARRISON TRIBE

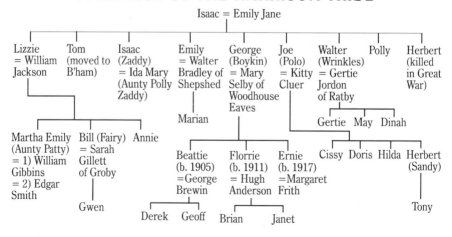

Isaac = Emily Jane

| Lizzie = William Jackson | Tom (moved to B'ham) | Isaac (Zaddy) = Ida Mary (Aunty Polly Zaddy) | Emily = Walter Bradley of Shepshed | George (Boykin) = Mary Selby of Woodhouse Eaves | Joe (Polo) = Kitty Cluer | Walter (Wrinkles) = Gertie Jordon of Ratby | Polly | Herbert (killed in Great War) |

Marian

| Martha Emily (Aunty Patty) = 1) William Gibbins = 2) Edgar Smith | Bill (Fairy) = Sarah Gillett of Groby | Annie |

Gertie   May   Dinah

| Beattie (b. 1905) =George Brewin | Florrie (b. 1911) = Hugh Anderson | Ernie (b. 1917) =Margaret Frith | Cissy   Doris   Hilda   Herbert (Sandy) |

Gwen

Derek   Geoff   Brian   Janet

Tony

*Mr and Mrs Walter 'Wrinkles' Harrison, with Gertie and baby May,
at 124 Main Street, 1914*

Gas came to the village in 1914, and those who could afford it had gaslights. It was seen as a wonderful new convenience, especially on dark mornings when, instead of coping with lamps, it was easy to strike a match and light the gas.

The heart of every house was the kitchen, which generally held a scrub-topped table and a grey slate sink. The more fortunate ones had a cold water tap. Hot water could be obtained from the kitchen range, which was also used for cooking. The front room was called the parlour, and was often used as a tea room for visitors to Bradgate Park. Everyone had a sofa – often a scratchy horse-hair thing. Those with a leatherette sofa considered themselves lucky. The parlour table was often scrub-topped, like the one in the kitchen, but it was always covered with a chenille cloth with bobbles round the edge, and surmounted by a centrepiece. This could be a stuffed bird, or maybe a beaded cushion, covered with a glass dome. The mantelpiece was often also covered with a chenille or velvet drape.

A zinc bath hung on an outside wall. On Friday night it was brought in and everyone took turns having a bath. In some families, friends were warned not to come round to the back door on Fridays, in case father was having his bath.

There was a closet down the yard. In A J's young days the pans were collected once a month (on a Friday evening after the pub was closed) by Mr Brewin and his team with a horse and dray. They made as much noise as they could, and set all the dogs barking. Being local lads, the Night Soil Men used to play tricks on people – hanging a dead hen inside the door, or fixing up a 'ghost' on the privy. The pans were then emptied on ploughed land at the sewage field on Groby Lane, opposite the place where the footpath is higher than the road. Later Zaddy Harrison and Fairy Jackson made weekly Friday night collections.

In the more remote parts of the parish householders had to make their own arrangements for disposing of sewage. At Blakeshay Farm the privy contained a row of five seats – four for adults and one for a child. Several farms had multiple seats, as the privies in outlying areas only got emptied about once a year, so the more alternatives the better. Water closets were only introduced in the 1930s, when mains water came to the village.

Haymaking at Poultney Cottage Farm, before the first world war. The group includes Joseph Crooks (centre), Wilfred (boy with pitch fork), Catherine (without hat) and Isabel (far right).

Location of pumps:

Public pumps in Main Street: opposite Vine Cottage (still there but not working); on same side of the road at Top End, opposite Brewins' farm (now removed).

Some private pumps: Old Post Office Row (there were four between three houses, but one was condemned); Thatched Roofs (at the front); Yew Tree Cottage; one for the row of three cottages opposite the school; at the back of Gable Cottage; Workhouse Row (one between three houses); Estate Office (two – one outside and one in the kitchen over the sink); Mrs Cordon's and Mrs Mossop's (the two cottages opposite the car park); pumping station (now tea rooms); the present Post Office (in lean-to shelter outside back door); Beech Farm; the Vicarage.

The first main drainage system laid in the village street dealt only with storm water, and possibly some water from sinks. The pumping station was opposite the park gates and contained two wonderful engines which pumped the water up towards Sheet Hedges Wood.

Most houses had a wash house, or shared one, containing a copper or a gas boiler. Kitty Brown was born at what is now Marion's cottage, where there was a fireplace on bricks against a stone wall in the garden. A big iron pot stood on it, and for years, summer and winter, the family washing had to be done out there, until her father constructed a shelter over the fireplace, with wooden sides and a zinc roof.

Drinking water came from a pump, and was carried in two buckets balanced on a wooden yoke over the shoulders. There were two public pumps by the roadside, and a big well near the allotments, which were close to what is now the Johnscliffe Restaurant. Many houses had their own pumps, some of which are still in position. If anyone had problems with their pumps, they called in Mr Geary, the plumber and handyman (who also repaired bicycles). Some people took their buckets down to the brook, which they dammed to created a sufficient depth of water. There was a duck pond in the farmyard of Walton's farm (at the bottom of what is now Grey Crescent). Water was a precious commodity and never wasted. After the family wash the used water would be put on the gardens.

Monday was always Wash Day. When the children got home from school it was their job to fold the dry washing and put it through the mangle in lieu of ironing. Sheets were carefully squared up, corner to corner, and then mangled twice, with the rollers being tightened the second time.

8

There was a general terror of thunderstorms, especially after Tom Crooks' house in Polly Bott's Lane was hit by a thunderbolt which went down the chimney. It was said to have struck the brass fender, so some women ousted theirs. No meals were eaten during a thunderstorm; all knives and forks were put in a drawer, and all the mirrors and any other shiny things were covered. A door was generally left open so that if a thunderbolt came down the chimney it could leave by the door. Mary Matts' mother experienced this happening before she was married.

Mr and Mrs Joseph Crooks and family, at Poultney Cottage Farm.

Most of the cottages had very large gardens, and many of the men also had an allotment at the bottom of Sharpley Hill. As the village was entirely owned by the Bradgate Estate, the allotments (like the houses) had to be rented from the Estate Office. The whole family worked on the gardens. Fathers concentrated on vegetables and fruit, while the women looked after the front gardens and took a pride in their flowers – hollyhocks, gypsophilla, lilies and roses are specially remembered. Children took it for granted that they would help wherever they could.

Most families owned a pig in a pigsty, and would scrub it with a scrubbing brush. When it was killed by the butcher, the children took plates of fry round to the neighbours who had brought their potato peelings and other scraps, and to other pig owners who brought their fry in return.

Children's clothes were usually home-made. Girls wore pinafores with a starched top and a frill at the bottom. Everyone had Sunday-best clothes, including hat and shoes. Florrie always had to show herself to her Auntie Lizzie before she wore a new dress to Sunday School. Last year's Sunday-best was relegated to second-best, and so on each year till it was fit only for working or gardening. Children's clothes were handed down to brothers, sisters and cousins.

For special occasions there were dressmakers in the village, such as Miss Warner, who made Florrie's confirmation dress. Later there was Mrs Butler, who lived in the Sunday School with her family until they got a Council House.

No woman would think of going out without wearing a hat. Wool or chenille hats were home-made, either knitted or crocheted. Felt or straw hats were bought in Leicester, either from a stall on the market or from Grices in High Street, which was Newtown's favourite store.

There were no proper shops in Newtown until just before the Second World War, when Mrs Bowler turned her front room into a general store, though several houses sold sweets, pop and cigarettes.The lack of shops was no great handicap, for it was the tradesmen rather than the customers who did most of the travelling. Simpkin & James from Loughborough delivered groceries, as did Burtons of Anstey. Bread came from several places, including Squires of Woodhouse Eaves. Four different butchers came round; there was little choice but always good quality.

Local farms supplied milk and butter. Johnsons and Brewins delivered, doling out milk into jugs and buckets. Even items like sheets and towels could be obtained from Stanley Harrison of Ratby on his rounds, and paid for at a shilling or so a week. Shoes were usually 'rejects' from one of the Anstey factories, for nearly everybody had a friend or relative who worked there.

A few people travelled to Leicester regularly (sometimes on foot), but mostly a trip to the town was a rare event. Reynolds ran a double-decker two-horse brake on Wednesdays and Saturdays from the present village Post Office to the Salmon Inn in Butt Close Lane, returning at four o'clock.

Regular transport for trippers coming out to Bradgate from Leicester began early in the century, with a horse-brake which started at the Horse and Jockey in Great Central Street. This was run by Percy Matts and his nephew Harry Allen. On occasion, they even took trippers to the seaside.

The first motor buses through Newtown appeared in the late 1920s and were run by Warners of Markfield to take people to work in Anstey. Before long a number of different bus companies started up, such as Huttons of Anstey, Allens (which were blue) and Parrs (green). The early ones were an uncomfortable ride as they did not have pneumatic tyres. Everard's brewery ran a steam lorry with a fire underneath.

THE CLUERS

John Cluer came with his wife and older children from Costock in Nottinghamshire in the later part of the nineteenth century, to be the village blacksmith. They lived in the left-hand half of what is now Marion's cottage, and eventually had seven children: William, Sarah, Kate, Nellie, Constance, Annie and Jack. The oldest son, William, was 14 or 15 years old when their father got a rusty nail in his foot and developed lockjaw. He was

The Cluer Family.

taken to the Leicester Royal Infirmary, but died there in 1890. Most of the children were too young to help their mother financially, but William had left school, and Sarah, aged thirteen, had just begun work at the framework knitting 'factory' in the white house opposite their cottage, where socks and stockings were made. Their mother, who was a tiny little woman, used to trudge over the fields to Bradgate House to work as a cleaner, and when she could, she would bring home left-over food for the children – as much as she could carry. It was a great treat on Sundays when they could have half a pig's cheek for dinner. Not that Sundays were a day of rest for Mrs Cluer, who was busy providing teas for Bradgate visitors.

There was no electricity, of course, and the cottage did not have gas. Neither did it have its own water supply. All the water for family use, and for teas for visitors, had to be fetched from the well across the road at Mrs Mossop's. Mrs Cluer had a few bricks outside, near the wall, where she lit a wood fire and boiled water in large black kettles for the visitors. For family use, she heated water on the fire indoors.

Despite being such a large family, they all had to somehow fit into two bedrooms. Later, when the children had married and left home, Sarah's daughter Phyllis used to cycle out from Anstey to spend weekends with her grandmother. There was a lamp downstairs, but when Phyllis wanted to read in bed, she had to do so by the light of a candle. Mrs Cluer died at the age of 67. William went to live at Birmingham; Sarah, Nellie and Constance to Anstey; Annie went initially to Leicester; but Kate and Jack stayed in Newtown after their marriages.

Kate eventually lived in a stone cottage higher up the village, where she also provided teas. The previous occupant of her house had been a very eccentric old lady named Mrs Warner, who used to walk into Leicester every Wednesday (there were no buses, and not even a road over Gorse Hill at Anstey) wearing a long purple skirt and blouse, cape and bonnet. She carried a large shopping bag and umbrella, which she waved about as she went, frightening all the children. For some reason, typical of village feuds, she hated the Harrisons and nobody dared mention the Harrisons where she was around. She often walked with the dozen or so Anstey children who had passed their 'scholarship' and had to make their way to one of the Leicester grammar schools each day. One of these children was Annie Lloyd, Sarah Cluer's daughter, on her way to Alderman Newton's Girls' School in Peacock Lane. She kept quiet about her own connection with the Harrisons.

Jack Cluer served in the First World War and worked for Groby Granite. He was cycling home down Groby Lane one day when he ran into something at the bottom of the hill, crashed into the bridge and was killed. Sarah met a young man who had come from the Forest of Dean to work at Bradgate House as a groom. They were married at Newtown Church by the Rev Kerry Williams on July 7th 1896, when she was 19 and her bridegroom was 26. Her bridesmaids were her sister Nellie and Minnie Rudkin, who later became Mrs Mossop. Her husband later worked at Groby Quarry until he was 65.

Annie Cluer became Mrs Drake, but after the break-up of her marriage, she returned to the family cottage and continued providing teas. She also sold sweets and soft drinks and stored bicycles for visitors and was well known to many Anstey and Leicester folk. Young people from Newtown and Anstey used to gather in her parlour on Saturday and Sunday evenings and have a sing-song. Annie never had a holiday; her recreation was to go into Leicester once a week shopping. Like most of her family, she is buried in Newtown Linford churchyard.

A J's STORY, (Alfred James Harrison)

I was born at Newtown Linford on 12 July 1902. My father was the local butcher, with a shop in the end room of his mother's house. I well remember my mother taking me to the new village school and meeting Miss Williams. I had seen the children through the iron railings at play-time, so I soon settled down.

When I was about six, my younger brother John and I had scarlet fever over Christmas. My father, being a butcher, was not allowed in the house. A large disinfected sheet was hung over the sitting room door and only my mother was allowed in for six weeks. She had a very nasty attack of neuritis of the head, neck and shoulder during this time, but Bengue Balsam eventually cured it. For our Christmas box we got a two and sixpenny clockwork train-set on a twelve inch diameter circle, plus, of course, apples, sweets and oranges. The neighbours sent in all the cigarette cards they could obtain, with which we made pictures in their correct series. I recall being taken into the garden for the first time in mid-February to see the violets and primroses. Dr Williams of Anstey came out by pony and trap.

At the coronation of George V in 1911 we had sports and races on the cricket field opposite Yew Tree Farm (where we went to live in 1914), and tea in the old restaurant on the site of the present Village Hall. At night there was a huge bonfire and fireworks on the Beacon.

It was either 1912 or 1913 when I was confirmed at Glenfield Church; my proud mother took me to Newtown Church for my first communion the following Easter Sunday. At breakfast afterwards my parents gave me a beautiful text, written in Old English lettering, and in a silver frame:

> Count not the passing years, but rather weigh
> The task attempted every closing day.
> Life is not theirs who know not how to live,
> Who strive to gather, but forget to give.
> He liveth best who, though his days be few,
> Renders to God and man a service good and true.

It was by my bedside for years, but stolen by a burglar who was obviously more interested in the frame than the words.

From 1914 to 1917 I attended the Newarke Secondary School, then a mixed school, in Newarke Street, Leicester. Our vicar, the Rev Bradyll Johnson, advised my parents to pay for me and not let me take the scholarship exam as he thought the paying pupils were put in a higher form than the scholarship children. It was the exact opposite! My parents had to pay four guineas a year and I entered 3 Lower, while the scholarship boys went into 3 Upper. At the end of the first term I was top of the form and moved into 3 Upper. My friend Ronald Alexander of Anstey, with whom I cycled to school, was top of 3 Upper, and for the rest of my three years he was always top and I was second. I never beat him.

In winter, if deep snow made cycling impossible, I had to walk to Groby and get a lift from the Everard's steam beer wagon which arrived at Groby Church from Burton-on-Trent at 8.10. The beer wagon always pulled up for water at the brook just before Glenfield crossroads (where there is still a Water for Steam Engines sign) before going up Gallimore's hill. If I missed Everards, I had to run to catch the 8.40 train from Glenfield station to West

Bridge. I could sometimes get a lift back with Mr Satchell of Clarke & Satchell, booksellers in Hotel Street, who lived at Lenthill Farm. He stabled his pony at the Fish & Quart in Churchgate. If I was there by 4.30 he would give me a ride home provided I walked up the hills.

Mr Gater, who was in charge of the boys at school, suggested on my first morning that I should ask my mother for a change of clothing to keep in his office so that I had something to change into if I got wet. I was glad to do this many times, although my mother also bought me a very large black oilskin coat from Thomas's store in Northampton Square.

At school the masters called me Harrison, but to the boys I was always 'Newtown'. My closest friend was Edwin Curry, whose father had a bicycle shop in High Street and a workshop in the yard at their house in Narborough Road. (They eventually sold out to Dixons.) Curry was always experimenting and we had several accidents in the chemmy lab. We made several cats' whisker radio receivers in match boxes and managed to obtain a pair of ex-army headphones. Edwin spent summer weekends with my brother and me in a tent at the top of our field near Bradgate Park wall. My father had a key to the Tyburn gate, and we used to sling an aerial between two of the tallest trees in Tyburn spinney and listen to the first Saturday evening 2L0 radio broadcasts – the Savoy Orpheans and Savoy Havannah bands and later the Fox Trot band.

In 1916 John Shakespear and David McTurk held their regular auction sale of stock and implements at the rear of the Bradgate Arms and in the cricket field. I was there in my school cap with my father, whom Mr Shakespear knew well from the cattle market. He asked me if I was good at figures and could book for him. I did. After each ten lots I ran with the slips to the cashier, Mr Edwards, in the pub, and was back to book the next lot. Mr Shakespear told Mr Edwards to give me sixpence – not bad pay for one afternoon – and told me to see him when I left school. That was my first experience of booking auctions.

I left the Newarke in July 1917 and for two months helped my father felling trees all round Cropston Reservoir for pit props. Things were bad, the war was bad. Labour was very scarce and I had been recommended by the school for several jobs with solicitors, accountants, Boston Blacking Co, the Engineer and Surveyor at the Town Hall, Faire Bros, Stead and Simpson, British United etc. On 29 September I received a note from Mr Haslegrave asking me to be at Warner, Sheppard & Wade, the estate agents, to see Mr Burton at 3.30 that afternoon. On Monday, 1st October, I started there at 8.30 as a five shilling a week office boy. I was 15 and could not reach the (one and only) telephone, which was on the wall of the general office. I had to beg a box from the wholesale grocers next door to stand on. In the 1920s I prepared the sale particulars and plans for the sale of the Bradgate Estate. I lived at Newtown until 1928, and in 1936 I founded my own practice as A J Harrison, Chartered Surveyor.

CHILDHOOD DAYS

Until the present school was opened in 1907 children attended classes in the Sunday School at the entrance to Bradgate Park. Gwen's father, who was born in 1896, was a pupil there, and told of tricks which were played on new boys, especially on April Fools' Day. His own ordeal was to be sent across the road to Mrs Cordon's at the white house to ask her for some pigeon milk!

Maybe the most dramatic escapade was when an unpopular woman teacher was 'tinpanned'. Lord Harrington's Hounds met outside the Bradgate Hotel several times during the season, and the children were usually let out of school to join in the excitement. When the new teacher refused permission, some of the boys absconded and followed the hounds. The next day there was a great row, but the boys were unrepentant. The rest of the school were on their side, so next day all the children took tin pans to school and set up a great row until the teacher left, never to return!

In A J Harrison's schooldays, too, boys sometimes followed the hunt into the park and 'forgot' to return. They would pay the price with the cane the next morning. A J remembers watching Lord Harrington dress for the hunt by donning a leather coat and then two or three more coats.

Huntsmen and Hounds passing High Acres, Main Street.

A J was one of the first pupils at the new village school, where Miss Williams, a very stern lady, was the headmistress. His father went to the old school as a young boy, until, from the age of about ten, he used to walk to Groby school. A J's mother was a pupil at a school for young ladies run by Miss Ball (later Mrs Snartt) at the farm next to the new school, and for which her parents had to pay twopence (2d) a week.

The new school building was well established by the time five-year-old Florrie attended from 1916 to 1925. There were sixty-eight children in two classes, and both the teachers lived in the village. The head, by then, was Miss Garner, who taught the seniors and boarded with Miss Annie Brown. During the First World War the infants were taught by Mrs Naylor, whose husband kept a garage in Anstey Nook. She was very strict and always had a cane in her hand, with which she used to rap the children's hands. Sometimes she clapped their ears with a book, especially if they were caught telling fibs. She would stick stamp paper over children's mouths to stop them talking, and a naughty child would have to stand in the corner with a book on his head. Her ex-pupils maintain they learned a lot, though.

First thing every morning there was the Register. Children answered "Present, Miss" when their names were called. The teacher's desk was in the warmest place in the room, at the side of the big open fire. The fire was made up with huge pieces of coal in the morning, and no-one can remember it ever being made up again during the day. Children were often cold, but were not allowed to wear their coats. Later a coke stove was installed, which was more efficient.

The school day lasted from 9 a.m. till 3.30 p.m. with a dinner break from 12.00 till 1.00. Every day started with a hymn and prayer, then half an hour's Scripture. The other subjects were mostly the three Rs, plus history, geography, Nature Study and Needlework. Older boys and girls went to Anstey once a week to do carpentry and cookery respectively. Young children wrote on slates, progressing to pencil and paper when they were more proficient.

School Orchestra, c. 1908. Back row: Noel Reynolds, Annie Brown, teacher; Bill Jackson, Gwen Charlesworth, unknown boy, music teacher. Middle row: Miss Wheeler, Adelaid Bland, Doris Brown, Eadie Freeman, Miss Brown. Front Row: Doris Neale, Daisy Richardson, Teddy Hill, A J Harrison.

Children who were considered responsible were made monitors. This was a great honour. The ink monitor had to make the ink by mixing blue and red powder with water. Every Monday morning she had to fill the ink wells on the desks; if she had added too much water, everyone's writing would be very faint all week. On Friday afternoon, the ink monitor washed out all the ink wells ready for refilling next week.

Other monitors fetched materials from the stockroom for the teachers. In Florrie's time it was a monitor who pulled the rope to ring the great school bell, in its tower on the roof, to call the scholars to their lessons. In later years this coveted task was taken away from the children, and only teachers ever rang the bell.

There were two children to a desk, and once they were seated they never got up again until play-time, unless they put up their hand for permission to 'leave the room.' There was no mains water or sewage at the school, of course, until it came to the rest of the village, so the toilets were pan closets in the school yard.

The yard was divided in two; girls played on the left, near Gable Cottage, and boys on the right, and they each went into school by the door on their own side. The paddock was surrounded by high wire netting, and was only used for organised games, not at playtime.

At dinnertime, children who lived nearby went home, and the others brought sandwiches. For drinks, there was water from the pump in the schoolyard. Later, when Gwen's mother was school caretaker, children would sometimes bring a cooked meal in an enamel basin with a lid, which Mrs Jackson would heat up on a big gas stove in what is now the office. Gwen remembers one boy saying to the headmistress, "Miss Everard, I've got a jelly for my dinner. Do you think Mrs Jackson will put it in the oven and hot it?"

Children were not restricted to school premises in their dinner break. After they had eaten their sandwiches, some of them would go off and play on Bradgate Park. With no watches, and no church clock in those days, they would lose all idea of time until the sound of the school bell sent them scurrying back down the village, late for afternoon school and duly punished.

Miss Everard was another teacher who used to rap the backs of children's hands, but she used a ruler. Gwen can't remember anybody being caned at Newtown school while she was there; she didn't come across this form of punishment till she went on to South Charnwood. Evelyn Callis, who lived on the fringe of Newtown parish, went to Markfield School as it was nearer to her house. She had a teacher who wore a thimble on her

Schoolchildren 1928
Back row: Rose Bland, Richard Walton, Norman Bland, Alfred
Smith, Robert Smith, George Such.
Front Row, Mary Matts, Doris Buthaway, Winifred Foulds, Dinah
Harrison, Effie Crooks, Ida Woodford.

middle finger and used to tap it, painfully, onto the top of children's heads.

Every Christmas, Charlie Walton, who lived at the farm opposite Newtown school, used to provide the children with a sack of oranges. Each child received at least one and sometimes two oranges. He continued to make this gift even when he left the village.

Country dancing was a great favourite lesson, especially with the girls. The schoolchildren, and those who had recently left, danced for visitors on the lawn in front of Johnscliffe café, which opened in November 1928. Johnscliffe, which provided just tea and scones, was built for Miss Halford from Blaby. She had been a matron on a Boy's School, and her uncle lent her the money. The site was an open space which had been one way up to the allotments at the bottom of Sharpley Hill (the other entrance being via Lenthill Farm).

When school was over, there were usually chores to be done at home. Everybody accepted this, but there was still time for play: skipping, hopscotch, marbles, snobs (which were sometimes proper, bought, ones, but often just stones or shoe buttons), whip and top, tin lurky (an empty tin was put on the ground, somebody would kick it and everybody would run and hide), shuttlecock and battledore. This latter was mainly played by girls. The boys would put a button on a string on a door, rattle it, then run off. Once their chores were done, children were given a great deal of freedom to wander at will.

During the school holidays, Kitty Brown's father, who was an estate carpenter, used to take his children to the watermill near Groby Pool. They would have a picnic and play among the trees. There was an eel trap on the stream, and Mr Brown would collect the eels and take them to people like the Haslegraves and the Stubbs. One night he brought home an eel in a sack and left it outside the back door. The family were gathered in the Living Room when they heard a noise and discovered the eel, still tied in a sack, in the room with them. It had somehow slithered under the door, through the back kitchen and into the room where they were sitting. Father had to give chase and grab it, while the rest of the family scattered.

Parents, as well as teachers, tended to be strict, and children learned to do as they were told, or they would be kept in or forbidden treats.

Home medicines were a regular feature of a child's life. In Florrie's family, every Friday senna pods were soaked overnight in a big earthenware pot in the oven beside the fire. The next day everybody had a cup of the liquid, to keep them 'regular'. Bronchitis was treated with goosegrease plastered onto the child's front and back. Blackberry vinegar in boiling water was almost worth having a sore throat for.

Evelyn Callis's family believed in taking brimstone and treacle in spring and at the 'fall of the leaf' to keep spots away. She liked the linseed and liquorice which was produced if she had a bad cold, or looked as if she might be going to get one. She also had to have Scott's emulsion, which was cod-liver oil.

The children in Mary Matts' house were given Californian Syrup of Figs each Friday night, and a sore throat was treated with a linseed poultice applied to the throat. Her father swore by Carr's Fever Powders and these were produced for almost anything, especially colds, flu and toothache. Mr Matts knew P Carr Loseby, who manufactured them. They were sold loose in most shops, but Mary liked it best when they bought a box of about fifty

Young Gwen with her Auntie Polly Zaddy, outside her shop on Old Post Office Row, c. 1930

powders, each carefully wrapped in paper, because each box contained a small gift, such as a pencil, a little note book, or a calendar. Beecham's Pills were also a great favourite of Mary's father's, and if he felt a bit feverish he would take two or more.

Gwen used to have a little cube of camphorated oil sewn into her liberty bodice. Pregnant women took raspberry leaf tea for an easier birth.

Not many people went away on holiday, but some managed a day at the seaside. Groby Granite ran a train to Skegness every year from Leicester's Belgrave Road Station (Great Northern). Workers and their families could go, and Florrie, whose father was a blacksmith's striker at the quarry, went regularly for about eighteen years.

Each year the children put on a pantomime for the village, and on May Day they danced in the garden of Gable Cottage, next door to the school.

One highlight was always the Sunday School treat to Bradgate House, the great Victorian mansion built by the Grey family near Field Head, then tenanted by Mr and Mrs Everard. The children and their mothers went with the Sunday School teachers over the fields to the big house, where they had tea in the hall, then games outside, with a leaving present for every child. There was also a Sunday School Prize-Giving in church once a year, as there is now.

The second Monday in January was celebrated as Plough Monday, when the children dressed up and went round the houses singing. In A J's time there was always a turnip lantern, and the children earned a farthing or

two as they went around. By the time Gwen was taking part, in the 1930s, one of the songs they sang went as follows (to the tune of The Ash Grove):
Plough Monday, Plough Monday, when men go to plough,
Doll Durden, Doll Durden makes pancakes so new,
She burns them, she turns them, she makes them coal black,
She covers them with hen shit and poisons poor Jack.

THE MATTS FAMILY

John Shipley Matts and Charlotte his wife, with their family, farmed at Ulverscroft Priory from 1891 until his death in 1917, when the tenancy was taken over by his son Richard Harry and his wife Isabel. They lived there until March 1923, when they moved to High Leys Farm, Newtown Linford.

Charlotte, wife of John Shipley, was the grand-daughter of William Stenson, mining engineer and mine owner, of Coalville, previously Long Lane. He was also instrumental, with John Ellis, in having the Swannington to West Bridge railway built, to carry coal into Leicester.

MARY MATTS' STORY

I was born at Ulverscroft Priory in 1920 and in 1923 we moved to High Leys, a fairly remote farm between Anstey and Newtown Linford. The track, which could be very muddy, crossed three large fields, and the distance to school was over two miles. My mother thought this was too far for a five year old. However, the next year the Midland Red buses started to run to Newtown, so I started school at the age of 6.

Children who came from a distance (including later newcomers from the twenty-row) brought our own packed lunch and took our own cocoa or tea to be made for us by Mrs Harrison, who lived in the old thatched cottage by the side of the Bradgate Hotel. Two of us fetched the drink and the headmistress, Miss Bailey, watched over us as we ate; no talking, and we were not allowed to leave anything. After dinner we were allowed outside, and if we had a penny to spend we would trek off to Zaddy Harrison's shop in Old Post Office Row. For that we could buy a box of Marston's Snow Mints, or four aniseed balls, one large gobstopper or two small ones, sherbert dabs, liquorice, maybe a lucky bag... what delights! Zaddy was a coalman and chimney sweep, so there was not much hygiene there, and even less at school, where the only water was from a pump in the playground which we couldn't use as it had been condemned as unfit – dead mice and the like had been found in the well.

The lavatories were at the bottom of the playground and were the pan type, with newspaper as toilet paper, but as everyone had the same at home, no-one knew any different. Around 1930, we returned to school after the August holidays and found a drinking fountain had been installed and a tap with a wash basin! Gone was the privilege of using Miss Everard's (the new head teacher) bowl of hot water provided by the caretaker each lunchtime for her to wash in. We girls all lined up and waited till she had finished and then she would say, "You may use it now." There were about five of us.

Another wonderful change had been made: the old lavvies had been replaced with gleaming white flush WCs.

Our wonderful schooldays were marred by the death of a little girl called Olive Frith, who died of meningitis. She was about seven years old – a pretty, curly-haired child with a delicate waxy complexion. Most of the children went to see her as she lay in her coffin, but my mother did not allow it. On the day of the funeral each child took a flower to school and they were arranged in a big vase. We were disappointed to be kept in school till the funeral was over.

Most children wore passed-on clothing. Footwear was usually hobnail boots. Some were lucky enough to have shoes, but wellington boots were deemed to give you bad eyesight! We always changed into our normal boots at school; believe me, wellies were a godsend, and kept our feet nice and dry.

From the age of 11 the girls spent a full day at Cookery School in Anstey. Our bus fare was paid, but we had to take ingredients. We also learnt household management, cleaning and laundry from Miss Gardener, and really enjoyed the day away from normal school. I left school in 1934, at 14, and started to work for my family, receiving very little pay as it was expected of farmers' children to work at home.

In the late '20s and early '30s, things were very bad for farmers, and I remember coming home from school to find my father crying – very unusual. My mother warned me to leave him be and not ask any questions. It transpired that he had taken sheep to Leicester Cattle Market and they sold for the sum of 6d and 9d each. This meant bankruptcy for many farmers, and nearly us too. I don't know how my father avoided it. Some of his friends committed suicide, and others went to Canada and America, leaving loads of unpaid debts. Wool was almost unsaleable, fetching 4d per lb in the fleece at the Granby Halls sales. My father kept back a year's wool and sent it the following year, but received even less for it.

Milk was at an all-time low. When Wathes, who owned the Oaks Dairies in Leicester, closed, we had nowhere to send our milk, and in common with all neighbouring farmers felt the end had come, especially when an agent came with the wonderful offer of 4d a gallon! Cows still had to be milked, and this was fed to pigs or poured down the drain. No buyer could be found in Leicester, but in time a buyer from Uttoxeter was found. They wouldn't collect, so the farmers formed a syndicate and Mr Brentnall of Newtown transported the milk from all the farms round about. The milk was sold to this dairy for several years until things changed and the Milk Marketing Board was formed and things began to look up.

During the 1930s best house coal was around £1 a ton, and every May we bought a truck load of 10-12 tons from Meadows and Ottey of Ibstock to last the winter. For buying a truck load we got it a bit cheaper.

Cattle food could be bought cheaper than growing it; best barley flour and wheat flour for pigs and poultry was on sale at £5 a ton, imported from the USA. Most of our land went to grass.

Twice a year farmers in the district, from as far away as Copt Oak, brought their sheep to Newtown to be dipped. This was the law; Cooper's Sheep Dip was used, and it took place indoors, in a barn belonging to Field View Farm, opposite the pub. We children had a wonderful time with the penning of the sheep – perhaps the boys more than the girls – and were given pennies for our help.

Another attraction was the Newtown Sale – a sale of agricultural equipment and cattle, sheep and horses, plus any surplus household items and furniture. This took place twice each spring and once in the autumn. When the estate was sold in 1925, the auctioneer, John Shakespear, bought a site on Groby Lane, for use on sale days. The hurdles and such like were stored in a barn and other farm buildings which had previously belonged to the farmhouse which was bought for use as the vicarage.

At home mother reared chickens, ducks and geese, all incubated under hens, some to replace our poultry flock, some to sell to local folk and mostly for Christmas, when we had many days of killing, plucking, dressing and delivering to customers. They were sold for about 3/6 to 5/- (17 to 25p) per bird. Some of our pigs, sheep and cattle were sold to George Lowe, butcher, of Anstey for perhaps around 8d (3p) per lb, and beasts 10d (4p) per lb, pigs 5/- (25p) per score lbs (20lbs) if we were lucky.

Washing and housework was very hard labour as floors became very muddy and sometimes needed scraping to clear off the toughest mud. Washing was all done by hand after the water had been obtained from the pump, which froze in winter, and boiled in the copper, which had to be constantly stoked with slack. Clothes were rinsed twice, once in clear water, and once in blue water using Reckitts knob blue tied in a bit of old rag. Tablecloths were starched using Robin starch and they looked lovely when ironed, using a flat iron heated at the kitchen fire. The clothes were mangled in an old large roller mangle to assist with the drying.

All the farmhouse cooking was done on an open range, which heated the domestic water in a side boiler. The only form of lighting was paraffin lamps and candles. We were fortunate enough to have a telephone.

Prices around 1930

Libby's tinned fruit	6d (2p) a tin
Butter	10d to 1/- (5p) a lb. at Worthington's
Bacon	10d a lb.
Sugar	6d for 2lb. bag
Margarine	8d a lb
Eggs	8d to 10d a dozen
Beef – best roasting joint	1/- a lb.
Breast of lamb	6d each
Milk	3d a pint
Adult shoes/boots	10/- (50p) a pair
Lisle stockings	1/- (5p) a pair
Knitting wool	3d an ounce
Dorcas raytex dress material	1/- a yard

WORKING LIFE

During the early years of the twentieth century, most of the village men worked in one of the nearby quarries, usually at Groby, though a few went further afield to Cliff Hill, Markfield. Hundreds of men from Newtown Linford, Groby, Anstey and other nearby villages were employed by Groby Granite, on the lane near Groby Pool, and at the adjoining Patent Victoria Stone Works.

The Stone Works bought fine crushed stone from the quarry and washed it two or three times in filter beds near Sheet Hedges Wood. It was then reconstituted and made into white sinks and paving slabs. These were weathered for a year before being sold, so there were always great piles of them in stock. Everything was done manually, requiring a huge workforce, and the manager, Mr Stubbs, lived at Beech Farm.

Mary Matts' father, who farmed High Leys, behind the road to Anstey, allowed the Anstey men to cross his land as they travelled to and from work. Some of them, such as Wilf and Sid Poole, brought horses, which they owned themselves, and between them they made a wide track across the fields which was not a public right of way. Mary saw them every day and knew all the men by name.

The horses were used in the quarry to pull wagons, some of them down in the hole, and a local mineral line linked the quarry and the Stone Works to the mainline railway.

At 7 o'clock every morning a hooter signalled the start of another working day for both the quarry and the Works. It sounded again at midday – this time to warn that blasting was about to commence, followed later by an 'All Clear'. Occasionally cattle were killed by flying boulders during blasting, and the quarry had to pay compensation to the farmer.

The hooter sounded again at 5 o'clock for more blasting and knocking-off time. Stone from the evening blasting was not cleaned until the following morning. The gunpowder used by the quarry was stored in Sheet Hedges Wood, in a brick building surrounded by a metal fence.

(After the Second World War the hooters were replaced by sirens. By this time the quarry reached nearly as far as the Groby Pool road, and one of the employees, Alf Martin, used to stop the traffic with a red flag during blasting, and tell picnickers to sit in their cars.)

In a hard winter there would be days, or sometimes weeks, when the quarrymen were unable to work. There was no unemployment pay, but if Groby Pool was frozen they could earn a few coppers by setting up a stall where they provided tea and coffee and sharpened skates. They also kept a long ladder close by, and for a small fee they would rescue any skater who fell through thin ice by laying the ladder over the frozen pool.

Some Newtown men worked in the mines and cycled each day to such places as Snibston, Ellistown, Ibstock and Desford. Evelyn Callis's father worked at Ibstock colliery and said that once the men were underground they had to walk back several miles until they were under Bardon chapel. All the men either

WHERE THE MEN WORKED

GROBY GRANITE: Walter Harrison, George Harrison, Ernest Harrison (son of George), Tommy Ingram, Fred Buthaway, Bob Frith.

VICTORIA STONE WORKS: Mr Stubbs (manager), Dick Sewell, Eric Brown (in the office), Herbert (sometimes called Sam) Hill (odd job man for Mr Stubbs), Jack Cluer, Billy Ellis, and his son Jim Ellis (who was a carpenter).

MINERS: Dave Wainwright and Pat Conway (at Desford)

DECORATORS: Jack Walters, Edgar Smith, Jack Bland.

cycled or walked to work, and sometimes, if they were not too far away, their children would take their midday meal out to them – usually a wicker basket containing two basins, one for the dinner and the other for the pudding, plus a white enamel billycan full of tea. The lid served as a cup.

Some of the men in the village were tenant farmers of the Bradgate estate, and boys often had their first job after leaving school helping on a farm.

Some people were employed directly on the Bradgate Estate. Alan Brown's father was foreman carpenter, with seven or eight men working for him. The carpenters' shop and saw mill was sited just inside the entrance to Groby quarry. There is a sluice gate on the outlet from Groby Pool. The water passed under the road, through an eel trap, and down to a watermill. The sawmill contained timber-cutting equipment, such as a circular saw and mortice and tenon machine. As a schoolboy in the First World War, A J was several times told by Mr Joe Brown to open the sluice gate to start the large water wheel which would work the machinery. It was a great thrill to see it in action. Closing the sluice gate was a lot harder than opening it. There were two cottages and various other buildings near the mill. When ARC took over the quarry, they demolished the mill.

Some local men worked on Bradgate Park, but dry stone wallers tended to come from Markfield. It was the Newtown men, though, who were called to the Park at holiday times and on busy Sundays in a voluntary capacity to help with fire watching and crowd control.

The estate horses were kept in stables at the bottom of Groby Lane (now a house conversion). They were beautiful great Shire horses, and brought in the big tree trunks when trees were felled. They were looked after by Tommy Hornsby, who lodged with Mrs Freeman in the stone house next to the present cricket pitch.

When the girls left school, at 14, they usually went to work in Anstey, where there were Boot and Shoe and Boxmaking factories. Florrie hated the idea of going to work in a factory, but nothing else presented itself so her friend Ada Warrilow got her a job at Palmers Shoes. It turned out to be not as bad as she expected, for the girls were allowed to sing while they worked, and Florrie, a noted local singer, was soon caroling away and leading the other girls

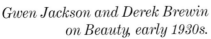

Gwen Jackson and Derek Brewin
on Beauty, early 1930s.

in the rounds that they all knew. She was paid 13/5 (67p) per week when she started in 1925. Seventeen years later Gwen, in her turn, also went to work at Palmers, but by that time Florrie had left to get married and bring up her family.

With work, as with school, Evelyn's story was different. Although she lived in the same parish, there was no transport into the village. However, she was close to the Ashby Road (the old A50) where there were buses to Leicester. She decided to go into the hosiery industry and travelled each day into town.

Local girls did not often go into service, though Alan Brown's mother, Nan Richardson, became a nursemaid to the Winstanley family at Braunstone Hall. If a farmer's wife wanted a maid, she usually had to look further afield and find someone from a more remote area. Factory work was better paid than domestic service and when you had done your stated hours your time was your own.

Kitty Brown did choose to do domestic work for a time after she left school in 1920, and became a daily maid at Beech Farm. From 1925 to 1967 her family ran the village Post Office from the front room of their cottage opposite the school. Her father was the official Post Master, but he worked as a carpenter, doing house repairs on the Bradgate Estate, while Kitty and her mother looked after the Post Office and Kitty did the deliveries. Her sister worked as a housekeeper for the Haslegraves at the Estate Office.

Tea on the front lawn, at Vine Cottage, late 1920s

A married woman's work was truly never done, for she had many tasks to attend to, in addition to looking after her home and family. Although a girl gave up her factory job when she married, she often continued with outwork, such as sockmaking on a Griswald machine for Morleys. Kitty's mother worked on a Griswald stocking-frame in her home.

In addition, there was the tourist trade. Before there were buses, people would walk or cycle or take the horse brake from Leicester. Most visitors to Bradgate looked for somewhere to have at least a cup of tea before returning home, so many women served teas in their front gardens and parlours. A plain tea of bread, butter, jam and slabcake cost 1 shilling (5p), while a full tea, which also included a boiled egg and tinned fruit salad, cost 1/6 (7$^{1}/_{2}$p).

*'Workhouse Row', Bradgate
Road (now demolished).*

Those who couldn't afford that
would bring their own tea, milk and
sugar and just buy hot water, so
most signs would read 'Teas and
Hot Water'.

There was a certain amount of
rivalry between the tea makers. In
particular the three ladies in the adjoining Workhouse Row cottages next
to the church (often pronounced Wukkers Row) were regularly to be seen
quarrelling among themselves as they each tried to drag customers away
from their rivals. Their cottages had no front doors, so they all had to wait
by the same gate, to the left of the Row. The card in the window of the end
house stated 'Miss Mee, Hot Water and Tea.' All the women wore aprons,
and one of them, possibly Miss Mee, always wore a navy blue woollen hat
with two peaks pulled down with a button on each side. The other ladies
were Mrs Fred Foulds in the middle cottage, and Mrs Sewell to the right.
Later Mr and Mrs Fred Foulds moved to a modern house across the road,
to which their son Fred added a café (which later passed to their grandson
Fred).

A J's mother started providing refreshments when the family moved
from 'up the bank' to Yew Tree Farm in 1914. If anyone enquired about
lunch or tea at the Bradgate Arms next door, they would be sent round to

Mrs Harrison. She also catered for
groups of schoolchildren and works
outings. These came by
horse-drawn brake and sometimes
the party would go on to Spring Hill
Farm, near Mount St. Bernard
Abbey. The passengers would have
to get out and walk up the hills.

Florrie's mother did teas, took in
washing, did paperhanging and
decorating, and helped with potato

*Tea and Hot Water.
Mrs Alf Smith, with Beattie and
Young Alf, outside 68 Main St.*

picking, as well as acting as assistant to Mrs Crooks, the midwife, who also did laying out. (The first trained midwife, Nurse Cousins who cycled over from Groby, arrived around 1930).

Evelyn's family lived too far out of the village to offer teas, but her mother also took in washing, and Evelyn and her brother had to return it in a wicker basket once it was done. Gwen's mother was always sent for to help with the washing and housework when a new baby was born. Many women went out cleaning, or gave special help with the annual spring-clean at such places as Pool House.

There were about ten farms in the village, plus some smallholdings, at the time of the sale of the Bradgate Estate in 1925, and everybody, even the children, helped at harvest time, if only by taking tea out to the workers in the fields. Farmers let the women glean the edges of the fields, just as in the Biblical story of Ruth. This kept the cottagers' chickens in free grain for several months and was also valuable to the farmer, for it prevented remnants of last year's crop seeding into next year's rotation.

Until the coming of the Combine Harvester in the 1950s, one of the local steam threshers (such as Bowley's of Loughborough) would be booked after the harvest by each farm in turn. During the Second World War the War Agricultural Department did the threshing with a tractor to drive the drum. Later Arthur Wheeler of Ulverscroft provided threshing equipment; his driver was Mr Storer, and later Neville Price of Bawdon Castle Farm.

For the children, threshing days were Red Letter Days. As soon as school was over they would gather round and watch the steam engine. The boys would arm themselves with sticks with which to kill escaping rats.

Three times a year Shakespear, McTurk & Graham held their popular Newtown Sale off Groby Lane. Cattle and sheep were driven in from

Haymaking at Beech Farm, around 1930.

From left: Eric Buthaway, Dick Sewell, Fred Buthaway, and Mr Stubbs (manager at the Victoria Stone Works).

nearby villages like Groby and Cropston, and even as far afield as Nanpantan. There was a big wooden sale ring in the field. After the sale the stock had to be walked home with their new owners.

Although there was a certain amount of wheat, barley and oats grown locally, most land was under grass and contained sheep and cattle, including dairy herds. Potatoes were not grown in bulk, but a farmer usually had a potato patch for family use.

A particularly local seasonal occupation was the stooking of fern (bracken) on Bradgate Park. Each farmer had his own plot to cut in late September or early October, when the fern was brown. A mowing machine was shared and an old horse-rake belonging to Harry Poole of Anstey was left in the Park, near the 'wide piece'. In return for mowing their allocated areas, some farmers would receive a piece of venison after the annual culling of the deer in February. (The rest of the venison was sold to local butchers, and could be bought at the Fish Market in Leicester.) Cutting the fern reduced the fire risk on the Park, and it was carted into the village to be used for horse and cattle bedding and as a lining for potato clamps. Farmers had fern stacks at the side of their haystacks, and manure heaps containing fern heated up particularly well.

Farming families sometimes enjoyed venison from deer which had escaped from the park. There were always deer in the woods, but when they were found in a cornfield, a farmer considered himself entitled to reach for his gun! In later years, when Florrie was married, her family sat eating Christmas dinner when they suddenly saw three deer in the garden, munching at the brussels sprouts. Her husband Hughie was not going to interrupt his meal. "We're enjoying our dinner," he said, "let them do the same."

One of the most important people in the village was the Estate Agent. He was the nearest most people ever got to Mrs Grey, who owned the village. At the beginning of the century, the Agent was Mr Garratt. He was very strict, and the children were terrified of him. At election times he voted Conservative, and made it clear that he expected the tenants to do the same. Jealous of their right to vote as they pleased, by secret ballot, most of the men (for women had no vote) used to keep their political leanings very private. One of the Richardsons, more brave or more political than other villagers, put up a Liberal poster. Mr Garratt tore it down. The next day another poster was in place; Mr Garratt took it down; and so it went on during the electioneering.

Mr Garratt was not popular, and Mary's father said things got a lot better when he left and Mr Haslegrave arrived.

Edward Haslegrave took over the 9,000 acre Bradgate estates in 1913 and continued to work until a few weeks before his death at the age of 84 in 1961. His brick-fronted house opposite the cricket pitch was the nerve

centre of the estate, and his office a total clutter of papers and books. Nothing much happened in the village without Mr Haslegrave's knowledge. He personified whole swathes of what later became Local Government responsibilities: housing, social services, environmental health, employment exchange. There were some notable bust-ups: there was nothing to stop him moving tenants around at will, and some folk felt that, in matters of housing, he favoured those who worked for him. But mostly people speak well of Mr Haslegrave; he would even let the young people borrow his clothes to dress up in for concerts and street parades. He was not a big man, and Florrie fitted into his suits quite well in her teens.

Edward Haslegrave,
Agent to the Bradgate Estate.

CHURCH AND LEISURE

Florrie's childhood Sunday consisted of Sunday School at 10, followed by the church service at 11, then Bible Class at 2.30 and evening service at 6.30. Sunday School consisted of hymns and stories and then the children were questioned on the story of the day. If children answered incorrectly they were told sharply that they couldn't have been listening. For the

adults, there were also Holy Communion services at 7 a.m. and 8 a.m.

Florrie went into the choir when she was 11. It was a good choir, with about 20 members, including about ten children, girls as well as boys. Mr Sills was the organist and choirmaster and the church would be full for special occasions, but not otherwise. (There were, after all, four services each Sunday).

There was a good team of bellringers, all men. The organ had to be pumped by hand – a rather noisy operation – and if left to go low it would drone. Florrie's brother worked the pump for some years.

Each May there was the Anniversary. This was an afternoon service in the Sunday School, where a platform was erected, and the children sang songs learnt specially for the occasion. The girls wore their new Sunday-best frocks, made by their mothers, and the boys had new suits.

By Gwen's time, in the 1930s, the Anniversary was held in the church and the children took part in the morning and evening services. At the practices the children were allowed to take turns at pumping the organ, but on the Sunday the task reverted to the expert.

The Sunday School, c. 1938.
Back row: Mrs Pigott, Rev. Pigott, Lily Goadby, Alice Frith, Rose Bland, Joyce Bland, Gladys Dickens, Mr Kirk, Freda Jardin.
Row on left: Tom Dickens, Tubby Atkins, Joyce Hill, Edna Dickens
Middle Row: Joan Frith, Patsy Patrick, Peggy Brown, Margaret Frith, Gwen Jackson, Grace Hill, Molly Brown, Gwen Hill.
Front Row: Arthur Reynolds, Avril Asher, Charmain Asher, Mary Naylor, Joan Mossop.

When the Harvest Festival came round the farms used to provide sheaves of corn and there were bags of potatoes, masses of eggs and vegetables, a box of coal and sticks by the door, and marrows galore – but not as many flowers as nowadays. At one time the produce was taken to the hospital, but later it became the practice to auction it in the churchyard on the Monday afternoon. The produce was piled up either side of the path.

On Christmas Eve, a party of carol singers from the church would meet at Florrie's mother's for cocoa, then set off at midnight to tour the village. First they went up the hill to Mr Squirrel's, near the Old John Car Park, then back into the village, singing at each house, and ending at the Vicarage at 6 o'clock on Christmas morning to sing Mr Pigott's favourite carol, 'Brightest and Best.' One night somebody dressed up as Santa Claus and appeared in the road as the party made its way through the village.

There was a well attended Mothers' Union which met one afternoon a month at the Sunday School. It was led by the Vicar's wife and Florrie's

The Mother's Union, 1907. The baby in the centre is Kitty Brown

and Mary's mothers were both members. There would be a hymn, a prayer and then a talk by a speaker. When Mrs Pigott was the leader of the Mothers' Union she would meet all the members at the church gate at 8 o'clock communion on Mothering Sunday with a bunch of violets. The Mothers' Union was eventually disbanded by a subsequent Vicar who was a widower, and who considered it was just a gossip shop. Later a Young Wives was formed, which, as the wives got older, became the present Women's Fellowship.

Florrie and Kitty were both members of the Girls' Friendly Society, which was a church-based weeknight activity for girls. They had Bible classes in the Sunday school every week. The GFS also used to take part in the Sankey evenings which were held at Mrs Snartt's farm next to the school once a fortnight in the 1920s. Mrs Snartt used to accompany the singing on her spinet.

Mr Haslegrave held a Garden Fete at the Estate Office each year in aid of Church funds. In his garden there was a full sized iron model of a deer, which had come from Bradgate House.

The Foresters' Parade, outside the Church.

The Foresters was a Friendly Society to which nearly all the adults of the village belonged in the days before the Welfare State. They paid their subscriptions and in return could draw sick pay and a lump sum to cover burial costs. At a member's funeral the men and women would form a guard of honour outside the church, with each person wearing a red sash bearing the word Foresters and holding a pole decorated with ribbon.

On Shrove Tuesday the children went to school in the morning, but at playtime they would dance around, singing:

Pancake day, pancake day,
If you don't give us a holiday
We'll all run away.

They were then given the afternoon off, and ran home to eat their pancakes and play with their new toys – a whip and top for the boys and battledore and shuttlecock for the girls; or sometimes marbles or hoops. Summer games began on Pancake Day, and from then on the children would be out playing on Main Street, blissfully unmolested by traffic.

Easter Monday was always special, for this was the time of the annual fair. People came from miles around for Newtown Easter, just as in the autumn they would flock to Ratby Crow Pie and Markfield Fair. All the shop people from Anstey and round about would set up stalls alongside the churchyard wall inside the entrance to Bradgate Park. There was no car park then; just a field with a road running through it. (Local lads would open the gate when a charabanc went through, and put out their hands for a tip.)

In addition to the stalls, there were roundabouts and coconut shies on the land opposite the Bradgate hotel, and the cattle sale took place at the same time. Maitland Hull's father, who rented 35 acres at Field Head from the Everards, used to buy in young beasts at Newtown Easter and have them ready to sell on at the October sale, or Loughborough market if they were ready for the butcher.

Maitland attended Newtown Easter on his own for the first time when he was four. Knowing his father had set up a stall, he took himself off down the lane from Field Head. He found his father all right, but got a cuffed ear for coming so far on his own. Fortunately, with a family of ten, his mother hadn't missed him.

Bonfire night was another special time, when people lit garden bonfires and got rid of their accumulated rubbish. The fires were kept small because of the proximity of thatched roofs and haystacks. Nobody had any fireworks, except perhaps a few sparklers, but children would sometimes make a guy by stuffing old clothes with straw.

For many years there was always a Boxing Day Whist Drive and Dance organised by Mrs Warrilow. Everybody went, whatever their age. The Whist Drive was from 7.30 till 9.00, then the tables and chairs were cleared away and there was dancing till 11.30, with music by Sid Partner and the Boys from Stanton-under-Bardon. There were refreshments at half-time made by the village ladies. Hundreds of pounds were sent to the Leicester Royal Infirmary from these events.

There were always a couple or so Whist Drives a year. The Conservative Party organised a Fur and Feather drive, from which the winners went on to a final at Melton. Before the present cricket pitch was created, cricket was played on land opposite the Bradgate Arms, and in winter the football team played on the same field.

THE BIG HOUSE

Everyone in the village was a tenant of the Grey Estate. The Grey family ceased to live in their mansion in the middle of Bradgate Park early in the eighteenth century, and let it fall into ruin. In the middle of the nineteenth century, George-Harry Grey, 7th Earl of Stamford and Warrington, built a new 'Bradgate House' between Groby and Field Head. It was the fashion to build 'calendar houses' with 365 windows, 52 rooms and 12 chimney stacks (thus echoing the days, weeks and months in a year).

Bradgate House, on the border of Groby and Newtown Linford.
The Leicester and Leicestershire Photographic Society visited
Bradgate House on August 18th 1917. This and the two following pho-
tographs are from the souvenir album they presented to Mr. Everard.

There is a local belief that Bradgate House contained 365 rooms, but that number of windows is more likely. It also contained twenty attics.

After the death of the Countess of Stamford and Warrington in 1905, the Leicestershire estates passed to her late husband's niece, Mrs Duncombe Grey, who let Bradgate House to Mr T W Everard of the brewery family. Mr Everard was about to be made High Sheriff of Leicestershire and felt he ought to have a residence in keeping with his new status. However, he always remembered his old home in Narborough with nostalgia, and on his deathbed pleaded, "Take me back to Narborough."

The main entrance to the house was by a white gate off the 'turnpike'

*Left: The Stable Block.
The Henstocks lived in the rooms
on the left of the gateway.
Below: the wooded grounds.*

(the A50), half way down Bradgate Hill. The area (now owned by Redlands) has become overgrown with the rhododendrons which used to line the grass-edged gravel drive.

Dinah Henstock was born at Bradgate House stables, where her father was coachman to Mr Everard. The Henstocks were a large family, of five girls and two boys (one of whom was killed in the First World War and is recorded on the memorial in All Saints' Church). They had a spacious eight-roomed house to the left of the clock tower in the impressive stable block (which had cost £30,000 to build in the 1850s). Mr Henstock was in charge of the stable yard, which also accommodated Mr Parrot, the head gardener and his wife – who lived on the other side of the clock tower – and Mr Timson the cowman, who had a smaller apartment. There were also two bedrooms for up to four grooms, as well as stables, cow sheds, coach houses and piggeries. The house was surrounded by picturesque woodlands, and Dinah Henstock enjoyed nothing more than to wander through the woods alone, looking at flowers and listening to birds and animals. Sometimes she would take a book and sit quietly reading under the trees. It was very peaceful.

There was a large staff at Bradgate House. Indoors there was a housekeeper, butler, footman, two parlour maids, a cook, three housemaids, a kitchen maid and a scullery maid, as well as local women who came in to help. Outdoors there was Mr Henstock the coachman, with three or four grooms; the head gardener and about five under-gardeners; the keeper with three or four people who worked for him, looking after the woods; and a cowman to do the milking. One of Mr Henstock's tasks was to look after the great clock over the stable arch, and there was a room over the entrance which gave access to it.

There was a parrot at Bradgate House, whom the butler had taught to swear. One day, in the course of a formal dinner, the parrot squawked out, "Who's a pretty bugger?" "What did he say, Arnold?" asked Mrs Everard. "He said, 'Who's a pretty begger, milady,'" replied the butler. Arnold was not quite as quick-witted as the local housewife whose parrot made the same comment during a visit from the vicar. The vicar didn't quite catch what was said, so its owner quickly translated. "He said, 'Do you take sugar, Vicar?'"

There appear to have been several parrots around the locality, all of them noted for their swearing. One lived across the road from the church and his shrieks could regularly be heard during services, but fortunately he minded his language.

The same butler and his assistant had a trick with a cork from a dodgy champagne bottle. Arnold would replace a good cork with his suspect one and hand the bottle to Mr Everard, who would immediately discard it as 'gone off'. The butler and his friend could then sit down with another good bottle of champagne.

The Henstocks considered themselves Newtown Linford people, as that was their nearest village. The children went to school in Newtown (the older ones to the 'little school' before the present school was built), and attended morning and afternoon Sunday School, though their parents would not allow them to go to church services until they were old enough to understand. They were regularly visited by the Vicar of Newtown.

The parish boundaries had never concerned anyone particularly until the marriage of Miss Phyllis Everard on July 18 1916. She wanted to be married at Newtown Linford Church, but no-one was certain about the exact boundary of the ecclesiastical parish. After research it was discovered that the line went through the middle of Bradgate House. Fortunately, although the back door was in the parish of Groby, the front door was in Newtown Linford. So as long as she left by the front door Miss Everard was entitled to be married at All Saints.

It was a memorable day when Miss Phyllis Everard became Mrs Logan. The smaller village schoolgirls, including Kitty and Florrie, were flowergirls; they had baskets of rose petals, which they strewed before the bride and groom as they came out of church. A J Harrison, together with his father and most of Kitty's family, sang in the church choir. Mrs Logan later lived at Pool House, Groby. The marriage caused some political tension in the staunchly Tory Everard family, for the bridegroom's father, J W Logan, was Liberal MP for Harborough. Miss Everard's brother Lindsay later became Conservative MP for Melton.

During the time he rented Bradgate House, Mr Everard had all the shooting on the Bradgate estate. He had four resident gamekeepers. Alfred Foulds, the head keeper, lived at Bradgate House Lodge. He had an orange moustache due to an addiction to woodbines. Jim Foulds lived at Sandhills Lodge, Ulverscroft; Mr Middleton looked after Bradgate Park, and there was another keeper who was responsible for Martinshaw Wood and Ratby Burrows.

Up to ten thousand pheasants were bred each year. A J Harrison and Harry Smith were paid sixpence a night for about two months in the Spring to scare the foxes off the young birds in the paddock near Bradgate House stables. Once or twice a week during the season, Mr Everard held shooting parties with twelve to fifteen guns and perhaps twenty-five to thirty beaters.

Beaters were recruited from local public houses, so men would try to be in the right pub when the call came out. They received about five shillings

Beaters at the last shoot from Bradgate House. Back row: Fairy Jackson, next to an unknown man. Front row: Mr Baum (Butler to Mr Everard), Arch Robins (landlord of Bradgate Arms), Jack Zanka (chauffeur to Mr Everard), Arthur Hull (landlord of Coach & Horses, Markfield), Teddy Walsgrove (landlord of Bulls Head, Ratby).

(25p), plus as much food and drink as they wanted, and a pair of rabbits. And it was not unknown for a beater to throw a brace of pheasants into a ditch to pick up later.

During A J's Christmas holidays from the Newarke School, between 1913 and 1917, he used to carry and load for various 'guns', particularly Dr Marriott of Leicester Royal Infirmary (after whom Marriott's Ward is named). He had to stable Dr Marriott's pony and carry and load for him, for which he was paid half a crown (12$^{1}/_{2}$p) a day plus a free lunch.

Dr Marriott would only use brass-cased cartridges, as these were safer. A J used to collect the empties and flog them at school for twopence each. He and Edwin Curry made some into cigarette lighters, using wheels and spares made in Curry's workshop. These were sold in Curry's High Street shop for two shillings (10p) each.

Maitland Hull's father was landlord of the Coach and Horses at Field Head. Although the Everards kept a good many hunters, when they wanted a working horse, they had to borrow one from the pub. When Maitland was old enough, he used to take the horse down every Saturday morning to the Head Keeper's bungalow by the workmen's entrance. The horse and cart took feed to various places in the woods for the pheasants, which were reared from day-old chicks. Payment for the use of the horse was not in money, but in kind – loads of hay, firewood or fern. The fern was mown from the woodland drives, which were lined with rhododendrons. Young Maitland received 7/6 (37$^{1}/_{2}$p) for his work, which was good money, especially as he also received an excellent dinner in the tack room. Mrs Foulds was a wonderful cook.

1914-18 WAR

The first impact of war on the twelve-year-old A J Harrison, was when, shortly after its outbreak in August 1914, men came into the village to requisition all the horses, except those which were lame or very old. These were handed over to the military for pulling ambulances, guns and as transport. It seemed very strange in the village without the horses.

Before long, very heavy casualties were being reported from the front, and there were constant appeals for more recruits (conscription was not introduced until 1916). Most of the local lads over the age of about sixteen went into the army, and most of the girls joined the Women's Land Army.

A J was a member of the Newarke School Cadet Corps, and had to report with his bicycle two afternoons a week after school at London Road station. As there were very few telephones, dispatch riders were used to carry messages to the base hospital on Victoria Park, with details of what to expect by way of troop trains of wounded soldiers. They also took messages to the several large houses used as rest homes for the convalescent.

Evelyn, Kitty and Florrie were all small children during the Great War. Evelyn's father joined the army and when he came home on leave neither she nor her brother recognised him. They saw a man in khaki coming towards the house and ran in, shouting "Mum, there's a man coming!"

Ration books were only introduced later on in the war, to make the food shortages fairer. Before that, obtaining food was something of a lottery. Kitty remembers her brother walking into Anstey to get groceries from Widdowsons in the Nook and coming back with anything they happened to have. One of the mainstays was Gongs soup, which came in little cubes of various flavours.

There was no butter, just horrible margarine (far inferior to later margarine) and not much of that. The Brown family used to make tiny amounts of butter for themselves by skimming the cream off the top of the milk and shaking it for ages in a glass jar until it separated.

HOW THE CHURCH WEATHERVANE GOT A HOLE IN IT

It was 1916, and the two teenage sons of the Rev Bradyll Johnson were very pleased to have been given a gun for Christmas. They met up with the 14-year-old A J Harrison and two of his schoolfriends, Curry and Skevington, by Mr Reynold's shop (now the Post Office). The gun was passed around and admired. Then A J, standing in front of the trap house between the shop and Beech Farm, pointed it up at the weathervane and pulled the trigger. On his second or third attempt, and to his own amazement, the cockerel suddenly began to spin round and round. When it came to rest, they could see – with young eyes, and when standing in the right place – that there was a hole through the the cockerel. The boys were terrified that they were about to get in trouble, and daren't tell anybody what had happened.

However, the story eventually got around, but – inevitably – in an inaccurate form: it was believed that one of the vicar's sons put a bullet through the weathervane from a field behind Beech Farm (which would have been a much more difficult feat).

The hole was repaired at the time the church clock was installed.

Country people could at least grow their own potatoes and vegetables. Skimmed milk was available, for a penny for as much as you could carry, from Poole's farm. Kitty used to be sent across the road with the biggest jug she could manage.

People who kept pigs were well off; they had hams wrapped in muslin hanging from the kitchen beams. There were plenty of rabbits about and Mr Neale from Beech Farm, Zaddy Harrison, and one or two more, used to go out netting them. If they had been caught they would have been in trouble. Kitty's mother used to skin them, stuff them, then roast them in the oven of the kitchen range. 'Butcher Ike' obtained permission one year to slaughter a Bradgate stag for venison.

A J well remembers Leicester on Armistice Day in 1918. Girls from the factories flocked along Gallowtree Gate to Town Hall Square. He celebrated with colleagues by going to Miller's Café for coffee and a slice of their famous cherry cake.

Schoolchildren were given a half day holiday. Evelyn was too young to go to school but remembers walking along waving her little flag.

AFTER THE WAR

During the inter-war years, there were regular motorcycle races round Ulverscroft. These incorporated the watersplash on Polly Bott's Lane, and were a great spectator sport for villagers, especially if any local riders were taking part.

A J was given his first motor cycle by his father around 1919. It was a $2^1/_2$ hp belt-driven James. He had to run with it up steep hills, because the belt slipped. Many of the hills were steeper then, before the roads were graded, and were surfaced with dry, dusty granite, not tarmacadam. Later A J had a $2^3/_4$ BSA chain drive (one of the first with 3 speed gear), then 'Red Indians', a Harley Davidson, a Singer, and lastly his favourite, a Ricardo Triumph, always with Wakefield Castrol Oil, with its own peculiar smell. Mr Naylor at the garage at Anstey had two racing 'Duzmo' bikes which A J rode for him at Beacon Hill trials and at the Mansfield track.

The first car in the village was a Model T Ford, bought by Mr Harry Beck, landlord of the Bradgate Arms in 1919. (Like the Venus de Milo, the Bradgate hotel came to lose its Arms. There is a Bradgate Arms in Cropston, and breweries don't like pubs with the same name in close proximity.)

Ulverscroft was a rather upmarket area of large, scattered houses. Children from the big houses tended to go to boarding school, but those from the farms – such as Blakeshay, Polly Bott's, Poultney and the Priory- walked along Ulverscroft Lane to the village school.

Newtown itself was a more homogeneous community. Being an estate village until 1925, people considered themselves equal – even if that meant equally poor. The vicar and the estate agent may have seen themselves as middle class, but the villagers didn't seem to notice and were in no way in awe of them.

There was a tramp known as Old Black Charlie, who used to help farmers. His name was a puzzle, as he was always clean. He slept under hedges and made beautiful bouquets of wild flowers, which he wrapped in paper doyleys and presented to people who gave him titbits.

A number of rag and bone men would come through the village with a horse and cart. One always shouted "Ragabone a rabbit skeenick!" and paid a penny for a rabbit skin, which was considered generous.

Electricity came to the village in 1936. Wilf and Mary Buthaway were married that year and went to live in a new house on the Markfield Lane service road. The house was wired up for electricity, but they had to wait a short time, using lamps and candles, until the village was put on the mains. The Buthaways' house was the second one in Newtown to be connected; the first was Mrs Berridge on Main Street, and the third was the British Legion Club.

Although most people had gas lamps in their houses, there were no street lights until the electricity came.

SALE OF THE BRADGATE ESTATE 1925

In the years following the end of the First World War, landowners all over the country were putting their houses and estates on the market. 'England is changing hands,' announced The Times in 1920, and the following year it was estimated that a quarter of the land in England had recently been sold. The great estates were being broken up (many heirs had in any case been killed in the war), and Mrs Grey's decision to sell her land was part of this trend. For the first time since the 'decay of the Yeoman farmers' in Tudor times, movement of land was towards owner occupation and small scale landlords. For Newtown Linford, which had been an estate village from time immemorial, it was the biggest upheaval in its history.

A J Harrison and his colleague Freer Ingold prepared the particulars and plans for the Bradgate Sale for their employers, Warner, Sheppard and

Wade. They used the old wood and corrugated iron village hall as their office. They had a typewriter and oil lamps, but there was no telephone, either there or anywhere else in the village. They prepared the plans from Ordnance Survey sheets, and for fieldwork used A J's father's pony and trap and A J's own motor bike. The procedure took about a month.

Apart from Bradgate Park itself, which was held back until 1928, there were two sales. The first was of outlying properties and took place in the ballroom of the Bell Hotel in Humberstone Gate, Leicester, on Wednesday 27th July 1921. It covered thirty six lots, including Ulverscroft Priory, which was sold to Mr S H B Livingstone of Livingstone and Doughty, Hosiery Manufacturers, of Millstone Lane. Mr Livingstone died in 1927 and the Ulverscroft estate was put up for auction again.

Sir Lindsay Everard (son of Mr T W Everard of Bradgate House) was very anxious to buy Ulverscroft Priory Farm and Ulverscroft Pool, and instructed Sir Stanhope Rollestone to buy them for him. The farm was Lot 14, and was successfully purchased for £2,275. The pool, which was all weeds and no fish, was Lot 20, and was expected to make £500 or £600. However, there was another interested party – a Mr Roberts. Sir Lindsay Everard had not stipulated any ceiling on his bid, and when the bidding reached £4,000 Sir Stanhope, his face covered in beads of perspiration, and not sure what he was supposed to do, gave up. When Sir Lindsay discovered that he had not obtained the pool he was furious, and told Sir Stanhope to buy it from Mr Roberts. The new owner would not sell, however, and Sir Lindsay was left with the farm but not the pool. The pool and stream fetched the highest price in the sale, far more than any of the farms.

The second, and major, Bradgate sale, took place over three days in 1925. It included parts of Ratby, Groby and Anstey and the entire village of Newtown Linford, with very few exceptions, such as the cricket pitch and land adjacent to the Park. The Bell Hotel ballroom was packed, and the crowd included most of the tenants.

For the villagers this was a time of great stress and upheaval, and

Rear view of Gable Cottage, bought at the sale by Mr Hurst.

some who remember it are convinced that it was very badly managed from a human-relations point of view, though no-one is sure whether Mr Haslegrave or Mrs Grey herself should be the one to blame.

When news of the sale broke, Mr Haslegrave assured the tenants that Mrs Grey was going to give them the opportunity to buy their own houses ahead of the auction. This encouraged those who had managed to put some money by, or who could find ways of raising the few hundred pounds required, to plan for a secure future. But for some reason, it was later decided to go ahead with the public sale and let the tenants take their chance with outsiders.

The matter was discussed over and over again after the sale, as people tried to find an explanation for this change of heart. Some said that Mrs Grey had never thought the cottages would fetch as much money as they did, or perhaps things would have been different.

Some tenants did manage to buy their own cottages, and others found themselves with new landlords. For these, life went on much as normal as some of the new owners retained Mr Haslegrave to administer their affairs. They went on paying their rent once or twice a year, or sometimes monthly, at the Estate Office in Main Street.

A J's own parents bought a pair of white cottages (one of which had once been used as the Estate Office) in case they did not get Yew Tree Farm. But they did buy Yew Tree Farm. With sixteen acres of land, it cost them £1,050.

Mr Crooks of Lane End Farm bought his farm and then had cold feet and thought he had made a mistake; so A J put it back in the sale the next morning and

A Cottage Interior.
Thatched Roofs, Main Street,
photographed soon after the sale.

Jasmine Cottage, Main Street.

Mr Crooks continued to rent it.

There were others who were less fortunate. There was no such thing as security of tenure; if a house was sold to someone who wanted to live in it, the tenants had to get out!

Alan Brown was only two at the time of the sale, and his mother was pregnant with his sister Molly, so she did not accompany his father as he set off for the Bell Hotel in Leicester. She waited at home, hopeful that her husband would return with the news that Yew Tree Cottage was now their own. Instead, when he came back he had to admit sadly that he had been outbid. The new owners were Mr and Mrs Holland, who had an antique shop in Leicester. (Mrs Holland was a dignified lady who looked like Queen Mary, complete with toque and umbrella.) The Browns had to get out, but everything in the village was so unsettled, they didn't know where they were going to end up. At length they managed to rent Jasmine Cottage from a relative. This thatched, stone cottage became their new home and in due course they were able to buy it.

Visually, it was the sale of fields, rather than houses, which brought about the biggest changes to the village. Builders were keen to obtain land alongside the roads to Anstey, Groby and Markfield. There were no planning restrictions on new buildings so, as in many areas, there was a rash of ribbon development. The population grew and in due course the character of the village changed from being a close rural settlement to being a dormitory outpost of Leicester. Even so, the resilience of the local families was such that they continued to have an impact upon the social and religious life of the village and to ensure that the community remained anchored to its historical roots.

AFTER THE SALE WAS OVER

One outcome of the Estate Sale was that the Victorian Bradgate House was sold to a quarry company, who demolished it. They did not destroy the stable block, however, and the Henstock family continued to live there for some time. Miss Henstock recalls this as a very sad time, when she had to witness the destruction of so much that had been familiar to her childhood. Both her father and Mr Everard had died before the sale, but Mrs Henstock and her daughters continued to live at the stables until the end of 1927.

In Newtown, 1925 saw not only the end of the old estate, but an important beginning. In that year, Mrs Haslegrave called the ladies of the village together and Mrs Everard came along to tell them about the Women's Institute movement, which had started in Canada in 1897 and aimed to improve the standard of home-making. The movement was now spreading rapidly in Britain, and the Newtown women agreed to form their own Institute. Among the founder members were Mrs Warrilow, Mrs Joe Bland, Mrs Bretnall, Mrs Jenny Foulds, Mrs George Harrison (Florrie's mother), Miss Adelaide Smith (later Mrs Sills), and Mrs and Miss Cordon (the infant teacher).

Monthly meetings were held in the Sunday School, and the committee met for half an hour immediately beforehand. Florrie joined in April 1926. She was only 15, but the Girls Friendly Society had finished and her mother asked if she could join. Her father paid her

The WI presented a seat on Sharpley Hill, in 1939. From Left: Miss Berridge, Mrs Hopley of Lenthill Farm, Mrs Warrilow.

two shillings subscription. Three other girls joined at the same time, and the youngsters had to keep quiet, get the cups out, wash up, and wind wool from skeins into balls while their elders sat knitting. There was not always a speaker. In a cookery demonstration, local member Mrs Bretnall is remembered for whisking a sponge cake with her hand. Hands were much more used in baking in those days. When Florrie visited her Woodhouse Eaves relations she liked to stand with other children at the big barred window of Squires, the bakers, and watch the bakers with their hands in the cake mixture.

Twice Florrie joined other WI members on train trips to Southampton organised by the Leicester Advertiser, from the Midland Station in London Road. Each time they toured one of the great passenger liners of the time; firstly the Mauritania, and on the second visit the Lusiana.

The WI was very different from nowadays. There were fewer Institutes, less organisation, and no singing of Jerusalem. Mrs Jenny Foulds, who was president for a long time, would stand up and read some very short minutes. Then the rest of the evening would generally be taken up with knitting, talking, playing games and drinking tea. About a couple of dozen attended, ranging in age from teenagers to people like Granny Bland, Granny Crooks the midwife, and Granny Warrilow – who were probably nothing like as old as the youngsters thought.

In keeping with the aims of the organisation, attention was given to subjects like hygiene, safe food, and proper diet (a background not all the members would have had). There were occasional speakers, such as park-keeper Jimmy Middleton talking about Bradgate. Cookery was the favourite subject, but laundry (including instructions on the use of a gofering iron) and needlework were also popular.

At around the same time the women formed the WI, the men of the village also got organised. It was sparked off by their annoyance when they went along to the pub on a Sunday lunchtime, and felt they were pushed out by friends of the landlord, who had previously kept the Midland Hotel in Leicester. So in 1926 they started their own British Legion Club.

They bought an old wooden, tin-roofed hut, which had been a Tea Room in the garden behind Beech Farm, from Harry Neale, and transported it onto land bought off Zaddy Harrison by Mr Pettifor of Anstey Brewery. Zaddy became the first steward, and the money was repaid to Mr Pettifor as they could afford it. Gwen's mother used to be paid a shilling to hold Mr Pettifor's horse when he went in for a drink. In September 1928 a brick entrance and bar and another room were added in front of the hut, which became the function room until it was replaced by the present brick

Zaddy Harrison's horse, Beauty, in 1932, with (from left):
Bill (Fairy) Jackson, Zaddy, Florrie and George Harrison,
and George Brewin.

structure around 1960. Around 1970 the Club changed its name to the Ex-Servicemen's Club, and in 1992 it became The Linford.

The present Village Hall, the Bradgate Hall, was at first just a wooden hut with a zinc roof, and known as The Restaurant. The present structure was built by Sir Lindsay Everard in 1930. It was one of several such halls he built in the Melton constituency for which he subsequently became M P. (His election slogan was 'You work hard for Everard, and he'll work hard for you'.) The hall is now rented to the village by Everard's brewery for a peppercorn rent.

Peace did not bring prosperity. In 1926 Evelyn's father, who worked at Ibstock Colliery, took part in the General Strike. He was out for six weeks, and never went back to the mine, but got a job on the Ulverscroft Estate instead. During the time he was out of work, the family had rabbit stew every day.

They lived at the South Lodge to Ulverscroft Cottage, where Capt and Mrs Lillingstone lived. The Lillingstones had a green Rolls Royce and a chauffeur called Mr Price who had a green uniform, with breeches and leggings. In the early 1930s their son, Luke, came home from college with a new motorbike and sidecar, which was all the rage. He had the gates opened at South Lodge and North Lodge to make a circular route. With a friend in the sidecar, he drove out of the yard, through the wood to North Lodge, left into Whisker Hollow, onto the Copt Oak Road, left again at Raunscliffe, left once more onto the old A50, then back through South Lodge and down the drive to the yard. By this time, the passenger was so shaken than he refused to stay in the sidecar any longer, and climbed out. Mr Price the chauffeur was persuaded to take his place. Luke roared round his circuit a second time – but this time he forgot about the sidecar and crashed it into the wall at the side of a gate. The bike kept going but the sidecar and its occupant came to a sudden halt, demolishing the wall. The sidecar was covered in bricks, but fortunately Mr Price the chauffeur escaped with nothing worse than bruises.

Luke got up to all kinds of escapades, which were the talk of the neighbourhood. He became a captain in the next war and was killed abroad.

The late 1920s were difficult years for farmers. To make matters worse, in 1927 Foot and Mouth Disease broke out in cattle in the fields near Chaplin's Rough, towards Anstey. Mary remembers seeing the fires where the carcasses were burnt; huge loads of coal had to be brought in to keep the fires going for a week.

1935 was the year of King George V's Silver Jubilee. Huge drays of wood were brought in and a great celebration bonfire was built on the old cricket field. This was lit by seven-year-old Gwen and a tiny little boy called Derek Brewin (The two also subsequently lit the Coronation bonfire.). Afterwards there was a party in the village hall.

Money raised from the Silver Jubilee celebrations was used to buy some children's swings, which were erected on land donated by Mr Haslegrave, where the electricity substation is now. This was conveniently close to the school, and Gwen loved to rush along to the swings before school started in the morning. On the day she was due to take the 'scholarship' exam, she was swinging away happily when the school bell rang. She was high in the air, but jumped off and fell heavily, grazing her knees. So she had to sit the exam with painful, bleeding knees.

To *Mrs Jackson*

The pleasure of your company at
NEWTOWN LINFORD JUBILEE CELEBRATIONS
6th MAY. 1935.

Children's Sports, 2-15 p.m. in Field (opposite Hall)
Children's Tea, 4-45 p.m. in the School
Adults Meat Tea, 5 to 6-30 p.m. in Bradgate Hall
Adults Sports, 6-30 to 8-30 p.m. in Field
Social and Dance, 8-30 to 12-30 in the Hall

ADMISSION by this card only.—Not transferable.

By this time, children who did not pass the scholarship (that is, most children) went on to South Charnwood. Alan Brown passed the exam and his parents made what must have been a considerable financial sacrifice for him go into Leicester on the bus every day to attend the City Boys' School in Humberstone Gate (now used by Age Concern).

If a farmworker lost his job, he also lost his tied cottage, and this is what happened to a family called Butler in the 1930s. They turned to the Vicar, Mr Pigott, for help, but all he could offer was the Sunday School. The family were grateful for any roof over their heads, so they moved into the Sunday School, which continued to be used, with a curtain covering their belongings at the far end. They stayed until they were allocated the first council house to be built on Main Street. Mrs Butler used to do dressmaking.

Electricity, drains and water closets were all installed at about the same time in the mid 1930s, and regular bus services now brought visitors out to the park, as well as taking residents into Anstey or Leicester to work.

THE JACKSONS

Gwen Jackson (later Wakefield) was born in 1928 at the far end of Old Post Office Row, which was previously known as Bolton's Yard. She grew up as an only child as her elder brother had died of rickets when he was nearly one and her mother had three babies who were still-born. Her extended family, though, encompassed most of the village. The Jackson

cottage was the usual two up/two down, but also had a big pantry which ran along the entire length of the house. Gwen hated cleaning the pantry floor as frogs and toads often lurked there.

There were other livestock problems, for Uncle Zaddy Harrison next door kept ferrets. When Gwen was only a few days old her mother proudly put her outside in her pram, and found, shortly afterwards, her precious baby sharing the pram with a ferret. Mother wouldn't touch it, and went to fetch father. Father wouldn't touch it either, so Zaddy had to be fetched to take custody of his animal. Sometimes it would escape from its hutch in the garden and find its way into the Jackson kitchen by climbing up the outpipe from the slate sink. This

Gwen in her pram.

was cured when someone found half a cannon ball (as one does), and this was kept over the waste hole.

Gwen's father's nickname was 'Fairy'. When he died at least one acquaintance was amazed to discover that he was really Mr Jackson and not Mr Fairy.

THE BREWINS

Horace Brewin was born in 1908 in Lenthill Cottage, where he has lived all his life. His father, John, was brought up in the village by his grandmother and moved to the cottage towards the end of the nineteenth century. Horace was the fourth of five children. Lenthill Cottage and its semi-detached partner, Hawthorn Cottage, were thatched until a few years before the Brewins moved in. The story goes that a youth who lived at Hawthorn Cottage went up into the loft after dark to catch the starling which was nesting in the thatch against the chimney. Needing light, he struck a match, set fire to the thatch and the roof over the two cottages was soon ablaze. Estate workers repaired the damage, replacing the thatch with slates. At Lenthill Cottage a new kitchen wing and extra bedroom were added to provide accommodation for an under-estate agent. He did not stay long, and the tenancy passed to the Brewins.

Top End was full of children when Horace was a lad. On bright winter evenings the boys would play football by moonlight on the Brewins' paddock across the road from their house. They would stay there till Horace's Dad came out and called "Now you lads, it's time you were in." The Plough Monday escapades are recalled as being as much enjoyed by the older villagers as by the children who dressed up and went round the houses. In the days before radio and television, any kind of entertainment was a treat. The children shared the money they were given.

Horace remembers the cattle sales each April, May and October, which (until Shakespears bought their own land on Groby Lane at the 1925 Sale) were held at the back of the Bradgate. Cattle were driven in, and penned up in front of the hotel. After the sale they were turned into the field at the back and buyers had to sort them out and walk them home. Horace has driven cattle from Newtown to Leicester Cattle Market for Farmer Gould, who rented the Lenthill Farm land from the estate when the house was occupied by the Satchells of Clarke & Satchells Bookshop.

On leaving school, Horace became a bricklayer, and later also became a part-time farmer. A couple of years or so after he married Lil in 1945, they built up a milk round and became full-time farmers. Lil used to milk six cows by hand, and still has a crooked finger which was broken by a kick

52

from a new cow while she was expecting her son, Malcolm. Horace did the rounds on his bicycle, with a bucket of milk on each handlebar and a pint measuring jug with which to ladle it out.

When they decided to buy a van, it meant a complete reversal of roles, for Lil was the driver, while Horace had never got on with hand milking, so he brought in a milking machine. All the bottles were washed by hand, and were capped with a silver foil top, using a special gadget. New milk bottles, labelled with the Brewins' name, cost 10d (4p) each to buy, while a bottle of milk sold for only 8d (3p), so if a bottle was not returned the milk was sold at a loss. One day Viv Brown found a Brewins' bottle on the sea front at an east coast resort and brought it home.

Horace remembers Ulverscroft mill in use. Mr Draper was the miller and farmers took their corn to be ground between the two big stones. Wooden boards had to be slotted into the dam to allow the pool to rise. The coming of portable electric mills which farmers could use at home knocked the water mill out of business and it closed between the Wars.

Ulverscroft Mill in the 1920s.

MARION RICHARDSON OF MARION'S COTTAGE

Ida Marion Manderfield was born in Grantham Town Hall, where her police sergeant father had an apartment. Her mother died after her birth. Marion, as she was always called, left school at twelve and a half to go into service as a trainee cook at Harlaxton Manor. She came to Leicester as a young teenager, arriving in considerable trepidation at London Road station carrying a box containing all her belongings. She was met by a pony and trap and taken to her new employer in a big house at the top of New Walk. She immediately wrote home to her father to say that she wouldn't be stopping!

Her employers saw she was not happy, and within a few weeks had passed her on to Mr and Mrs Cliffe-Jones, who had a summer residence at

High Roby in Ulverscroft as well as their town house in Leicester. They kept two or three maids, a cook and a chauffeur, and Marion settled more happily into this household.

At High Roby, Marion made friends with a young man named George Richardson, a gardener who spent half the week working for Mr Haslegrave and the other half at Stoneywell, next door to High Roby. George, of course, had a nickname, and was known as Dido. He was a Newtown lad, born at the turn of the century, and one of six children. He claimed to be the first person in Leicester to survive a mastoid operation. He was about ten years old when he became ill, and the doctor came to Newtown in his pony and trap to attend to him. As George became more and more ill, the doctor prepared his mother for his death. However, he said, there was one spark of hope. He had been in touch with a London surgeon who had done an operation for mastoids, and he was prepared to come and have a look at the boy. The surgeon came to Leicester Royal Infirmary, considered the case, and agreed to operate. George was put under chloroform and the operation proved successful, though it left him deaf and with a hole behind his ear and a scar down into his neck.

According to family tradition, George remained in hospital for two years. During this time his mother used to visit him at the Infirmary once a week, taking provisions such as chicken, eggs, butter and garden produce. Sometimes she got a lift one way from Reynolds the carter, but mostly she took the gated green lane over Anstey Gorse, attended to her lad, then walked home again (a return journey of fourteen miles) to see to her other five children.

When Marion and George decided to get married, they needed somewhere to live. This was solved when George told Mr Haslegrave that he was engaged. "Bring Marion to see me and I will give you a list of houses which are available," he said. The young couple inspected the accommodation on offer and settled upon the right half of the semi-detached cottages which now comprise Marion's Cottage. The rent was one shilling and sixpence (7^{1}/$_{2}$p) a week, and the Cluer family were next door in the other half of the building.

Mr Haslegrave was surprised at their choice of a cottage he considered somewhat dilapidated, and set estate workers to renovate it. An outside WC was installed, and in the kitchen there was a copper and a black-leaded range for cooking and heating. Lighting was by gas.

Marion and George had a son, John (known as Young Dido). When the war came, people were not allowed to keep two homes. Basil and Muriel Gimson, who owned Stoneywell, lived during term time at Bedale School, a modern co-educational private school where Basil was Deputy Head. Stoneywell was therefore let to a gynaecologist, Dr Lodge, his wife and three children, who had been bombed out of their house in London Road, Leicester. George, Marion and John moved in with them for the duration: George as caretaker/gardener and Marion as cook/housekeeper, releasing their own cottage for other tenants. After the war everyone returned home.

Marion was very active in the community. She taught in the Sunday School, sang in the church choir, belonged to the Drama Society and was a leading light in the W.I. and the Women's Fellowship. She lived in the same cottage for the rest of her life, but when Annie Cluer (Drake) died in 1972, the Bradgate trustees offered Marion and George the other half of the house. They accepted, but shortly afterwards George died, leaving Marion in sole tenancy of what had been two cottages. She died at home, suddenly, in 1974. The Bradgate Park Trust did not re-let the cottage, but opened it as a shop and interpretive centre in 1976.

INCOMERS

ANNE GIMSON'S parents, Mr and Mrs Hurst, bought Gable Cottage, next door to the school, at the sale in 1925. They had a large house in London Road, Leicester, where they spent the winter months, but each spring a furniture van was loaded with mattresses and other belongings, and the family and their maids moved to Newtown for the summer. Anne's father, who was a very practical man with his hands, loved country life, and so did the children, but mother preferred the town, so this compromise was made. During the summer term, Anne caught the bus back to Leicester to go to school. Unlike the other villagers, the Hursts had the luxury of electricity from their own generator, which was underneath Anne's bedroom – so there was no temptation to stay in bed late in the mornings,

for once the generator was switched on, the noise and fumes made the bedroom untenable. At first water from the well had to be pumped up to the bathroom, and the children all had to do their stint of pumping each morning. Later their father electrified this process, too.

The dining room at Gable Cottage.

At the outset of the Second World War, the London Road house was requisitioned to be used as offices, and Gable Cottage became the family's permanent home. Mrs Hurst became immersed in village activities and no longer hankered after the town, so the family stayed on after the war as full-time villagers.

Anne exchanged one historic house for another, less ancient but equally fascinating, when she and her husband Don Gimson moved into Stoneywell Cottage in Ulverscroft. This stone and slate house has remained in the Gimson family since it was built for his brother Sidney by Ernest Gimson, architect, furniture designer, and a leading member of the English Arts and Crafts Movement at the end of the nineteenth century.

MARGARET TREWIN (née Tomlinson) came to Newtown around 1932 for the good of her health. A weak and sickly child who had scarcely had any schooling as she was always ill, she was taken along to the TB clinic when she was six. Her parents were told that she must be given the open-air treatment and live at the seaside or on Charnwood Forest, or she would die.

The family therefore bought a modern house on Main Street, in an elevated position overlooking the bottom of Markfield Lane. Margaret spent the next three years sitting on the front porch, summer and winter, and at night slept with her bedroom windows wide open at all times. There was nothing she could do except read, so she devoured every book she could obtain, particularly history and classic stories. When she was ten, the doctors said she could go to school in Loughborough, but not on any account in Leicester, which would be fatal to her. So at ten, she began at last to experience school, and was surprised to find that, except in Maths, she was not at all behind, for through her wide reading she had educated herself. She became fit and well, and has lived in other parts of the world, but returned to Newtown. In due course she became a Primary School teacher and helped other children through the school years that she herself had missed.

THE SECOND WORLD WAR

During the Second World War, queuing became a normal part of life; it was said "Any two, form a queue." People would walk the two miles to Anstey, queue for hours at the butchers and then find nothing left. As in the First World War, though, it was easier in the country than in the town, as people not only had gardens and allotments, but often fowls and pigs. A good deal of swapping went on: eggs from the family hens for somebody else's cheese ration, and so on. The acquaintance of useful shop assistants was carefully cultivated.

Those who kept pigs were allowed to kill two a year for home consumption, but had to give up their bacon coupons. Farmworkers were allowed to buy a medium-sized pork pie a week from Folwells in Leicester, and these were collected on a Tuesday by Mannie Hopley.

Coal was rationed, so Florrie (who was now married) and her family would go into the woods with a sack, wooding; her father would saw up logs on his bench. Everybody who worked on the park was allowed one horse-dray-load of wood per year.

Evacuees were boarded in the village. About a dozen children came from London and filled the school to overflowing. Gwen's main memory is that many of them suffered from Impetigo, and one child's vest was stuck to her body with it.

The Home Guard, 1942 (with first world war Canadian rifles).
Back: Edward Haslegrave, Harry Matts, Harold Hurst (Cpl),
Alan Brown, Jack Hewitt, Ben Shipman, Bill Jackson, Percy Matts,
Albert Wolf, Hugh Anderson, unknown.
Middle: Horace Boulter (L.Cpl), Jack Staniland (Sgt),
Gordon Fantam (1st Lt), Bill Lowe (2nd Lt), Jack Bland (Sgt),
Cyril Littleworth (Sgt). Front: Dido Richardson, Jack Oldham,
Ted Chaplin, Billy Stevens, Arnold Adkin.

The British Legion Hall, in use as a Dunlop Rubber factory.

A new activity for the young people, the Charnwood Young Farmers group, was formed around 1940 by Frank Stopps, manager of Leicester City Farms, and Mr Bird, their poultry keeper. The group met once a month at the village school, with Jim Neale as chairman and Josie Thompson as secretary. They had talks and competitions and went out to rallies. Mary Matts was a member, and Mr Haslegrave supported the venture.

During the bombing, people from Leicester sometimes came out to the village to sleep as it was safer. Evelyn, who was newly married and living on the Twenty Row in Anstey, put up several of her Leicester workmates who would come for a break.

Throughout the war, the village was virtually taken over by the military, and much of Bradgate Park was closed to the public. There was a First Aid Point in the Sunday School, hard-track vehicles were driven round the lanes and there were Nissen huts on both sides of Main Street. When the soldiers who had been billeted in them were sent to France, some huts were occupied by Scottish miners who were sent to work at Desford and Bagworth collieries. Other huts were allocated to people who had become homeless, such as Dan Richards, a teacher at Anstey, and his wife Kathleen.

There was a searchlight in a field in Markfield Lane, and munition huts all round Charnwood Forest. Local lads would sometimes break in and play 'fireworks' with them. Police tried to stop them, but nobody heard of anyone coming to any harm.

Very few bombs disturbed the village. One fell noisily but harmlessly in a four acre field near Cropston Reservoir during a September evening in 1941. It left a large crater in the middle of the field, with just a narrow edge round it. Evelyn was so startled that she fell over. Another bomb fell on what is now the Nature Reserve in Whitcroft Lane.

As part of the Home Front, a busload of women travelled one evening a

58

The British Legion 'factory' also served for more relaxing wartime functions. In more peaceful times it was a skittle alley.

week to South Charnwood School to prepare vegetables and make puddings for the next day's school dinners – unpaid, of course. When the Home Guard went on manoeuvres on Sunday mornings, some of the women prepared breakfast at the village school, and the Girls' Training Corps packed up their lunches. One of the girls put a poem she had written into a lunch box, chosen at random. The recipient sent a reply and a romance followed which led to marriage.

The tin hut at the back of the British Legion Club became a factory used by Dunlop for the assembly of aircraft parts. It had a manager, Mr Waldron, and about thirty village women, who worked there in two shifts: morning and afternoon. Florrie worked there in the afternoons, while her mother looked after her son Brian, who had been born at the beginning of the war.

The Women's Institute made its own contribution to the war effort. Members met in the Bradgate Hall to make pyjamas for military hospitals. Those who lived close by took their sewing machines, while the others did the cutting out. Mary made button holes and helped with any finishing off. Mr Haslegrave's sister obtained wool from which members knitted gloves, mittens and socks for the army. Parcels of dried fruit were received from Australia and these were raffled off at meetings; supplies of vitamin tablets from Canada were distributed.

Mr Hackett, who lived in one of the new houses at the bottom of Groby Lane, was General Secretary of the Leicestershire Co-operative Society. He had some large safes installed in his cellar as it was felt company papers would be safer in Newtown than in Leicester.

The end of the war was celebrated with a big free home-coming party in the Bradgate Hall for all the men and women who had been in the forces. Money was raised by socials and whist drives so that it could be a lavish event. All the ex-service people were photographed together on stage by a Leicester Mercury photographer, and to clear the remaining funds, a copy (shown opposite) was given to each person present.

MIM JOHNSON

There have been Johnsons in Newtown for very many years. Millicent, otherwise known as Mim, knows that her great-grandfather lived in the white thatched cottage close to the school where she has spent all her life.

Her grandfather, Tom Rudkin Johnson, and his wife Bertha named their son George Harry, surely after George Harry Grey, the seventh Earl of Stamford. Tom could turn his hand to either building or tree felling. He cleared four acres of Benscliffe Wood, and he and George Harry repaired the ruins in the park, built the kitchen extension to the Sunday School, converted the barns adjacent to Greystones into living accommodation and made the stone gateposts and bridge parapet at Linford House. At Beech Farm, in Freddie Upchurch's time, they changed the cowsheds into stables and back to cowsheds again.

Tom Rudkin Johnson bought his cottage and croft at the estate sale in 1925, but during the depression there was not enough local work to keep him occupied. He eventually found building work at Tamworth and travelled there each week, walking or cycling, and returned home for the weekend. He always kept some milking cows, and these needed to be milked when he was away in Tamworth, so he employed a succession of farmworkers who attended to the milking and also helped out other farmers as required.

Mim's grandmother, Bertha, delivered milk round the village from a horse-drawn milk float. Always nervous that the horse might bolt, she sat sideways so that she could jump off if necessary. At weekends, Tom and George took over the milk round on their motorbike. This had panniers at the back to hold bottles of milk, and when Mim was old enough she would travel pillion, holding a bucket of milk in each hand! On Sundays in summer the cafés and tea places would want two deliveries.

Millicent was born in 1934 and attended the village school until she was eleven. She admits that although she lived the nearest, she was usually the last to arrive, and had no interest in anything except the sport. She moved on to South Charnwood School and left as soon as she was allowed, thankful that her birthday was in August and not September.

It was getting more expensive to employ farmworkers to do the milking, so the fifteen-year-old Millicent took over the job. She milked a dozen or so cows by hand twice a day, and did her deliveries on a push-bike. A bag of bottles and a bucket of milk hung from each handlebar, and a frame held more bottles over the back mudguard. She had to cover the entire village, as she had customers in the end houses in each direction. The most frustrating thing was to run out of milk at the top of Bradgate Road and to have to return for just a few bottles more.

Mim's working day for many years was:
Up at 7; feed the cows, then a quick cup of tea.
Milk a dozen cows by hand.
Breakfast.
Milk deliveries round village (till about 12.30)
Quick dinner
In winter: clean out cows and straw down.
Second milking
In summer: second delivery as required.

Because of the tea places, there was much more demand for milk in the summer than in the winter. Excess milk was put out for the cream to rise, then this was hand-churned into butter by her grandmother, sometimes taking her two hours in the evening. Skimmed milk and buttermilk were fed to the pigs.

Grandma Johnson used to go shopping in Leicester twice a week, on Tuesdays and Fridays, and would walk miles from shop to shop to save tuppence. Mim reckons they were always the last in the village to have anything: electricity, television, telephone, car....

In the mid-1950s new regulations put an end to carting buckets of milk round the village. All milk had to be bottled. Millicent carried on milking, but the milk was now left out in churns to be picked up by the lorry from the Co-op Dairy.

Mim's grandmother, father and mother all died in quick succession one unhappy year, and she continued to live with her grandfather until he, too, died. Not that she was left much to her own devices: being next-door-but-one to the school, her farm was a favourite place for local children to congregate after going-home time. They would help, or otherwise, with the milking, haymaking and putting the cows out to grass. It was a second home to many. If they were hungry, there was usually something to eat; they indulged in water fights and mud fights, and picked up a multitude of useful skills. Some children were regularly banned by Mim for bad behaviour, but after a few days they were generally back. When they grew up and left the village (few local youngsters can afford to live in Newtown when they marry) they would keep coming back to visit Mim; some have said that the hours after school, helping with the cows, were the happiest of their lives.

On Friday, May 13 1975, Millicent vacated her cottage for a year for major rebuilding, and lived in a caravan in the yard. Soon afterwards, the dairies stopped collecting churns and went over entirely to bulk tankers. There was no longer a place in the scheme of things for the small farmer who hand-milked a dozen cows. Mim briefly flirted with the idea of finding a job in a factory, but decided she would go mad indoors, so she changed to raising beef cattle and took in horses at livery. No more village children learned to milk on their way home from school, but Millicent continues to be the first port of call for anyone worried about their horses, cows, cats, dogs, chickens or love life. Every village needs a Mim.

Mim Johnson's Cottage in Main Street. before it was renovated

MORE INCOMERS

JENNY WHITEHEAD and her family first came to live in Newtown during the Second World War, because their Stoneygate house in Leicester was bombed. At first they took refuge at Roecliffe Manor, where Jenny's aunt Eileen was matron of the Children's Convalescent Home. Then they rented a house on Sharpley Hill, near the Old John Car Park. They returned to Stoneygate when their house was repaired, but in 1948 it was purchased by the University College (now Leicester University). The family chose to move back to Newtown, and bought Ivy House Farm, which was in a very run-down condition. Jenny took up nursing, and worked in hospitals in Cornwall and London before moving back to the village..

VIV BROWN (née Tomlin) was brought up in Oadby, and was living in a caravan with her husband John when, in 1953, her father bought the house that is now called Linford Farm. Her mother was distressed at this turn of events, as she had lived all her life in Oadby, and had no wish to move out to what she saw as the back of beyond. To cheer her up, Viv offered to forego life in the caravan and she and John moved in with her parents and brother. She went to work in Leicester each day on her Vespa scooter; she was the first woman Vespa rider in Leicester, having bought the machine in Norfolk. Eighteen months later Viv and John moved to a house of their own in Markfield Lane, raised a family, and have stayed in the area ever since.

THE POST OFFICE HOLD-UP
Kitty Brown's Story

I shall never forget that day. It was November 30th 1963, a Saturday morning. My sister Lil was home. She had been scrubbing the steps, and mother was with us in the front room where we had the Post Office. From the window I saw a youth walking backwards and forwards, backwards and forwards. He had an air-force scarf wrapped round his face. I said to Lil, "I don't know what that boy is walking about like that for."

Then he came in, a gun in his hand, and said "This is a holdup! Nobody will get hurt if you give me some money." And he put a bullet in his gun.

People say your blood runs cold, and mine certainly did. I said to him, "I'm sorry. You've come the wrong day. The postman's just been." I had just emptied the telephone box across the road and there were pennies all over the table. I told my mother to fetch my brother, knowing he was no-where about.

I never thought he would let my mother go, but she went out by the back door and then went running up the yard. The lad panicked, pushed his gun into the top of his trousers and ran out of the front door and down the road. Rita from next-door-but-one saw him and ran to tell Annie Brown at the shop, who telephoned the police.

The police were very helpful, but the culprit was never caught. When it was all over we tried to do the Post Office accounts as usual, but none of us could concentrate. We had to leave them until the next day.

POST WAR CHANGES

New building and road widening continued to alter the rural aspect of the village. Groby Lane had been widened before the war, when the bottom part of the service road was constructed. It had been a narrow lane with overhanging trees, and the steep hill where the houses were to be built was dug out by local men with spades. The red clay was piled onto horsedrawn carts and taken away.

Council houses were built, first on Main Street, then in what is now Grey Crescent (then Grey Close, as it was a cul-de-sac). Those on the north side of Grey Close were for returning servicemen who had no-where to live, plus a Police-house for the resident policeman; those on the south side were for farmworkers, and provided a secure tenancy instead of a tied cottage.

The village became busier. Many cottages, as well as the cafés, still served teas. Walkers and cyclists still poured in on fine weekends, and cycles could still be stored for twopence at Annie Cluer's, but more people were now arriving (or at least returning, footsore) by bus. Alan Brown once counted twenty double-decker buses lined up outside the pub to take people back to Leicester. The bus queue often stretched as far as Markfield Lane. Those who waited at the bus stop nearer to the Park gates tended to see the buses drive past already full, so at busy times it was better to walk to the pub terminus. Sometimes a bus inspector would send a bus off empty so that it could pick up people on the way to Leicester as there were continual complaints about buses going past already full.

New houses began to fill in the spaces along the roads. The wooden shacks on Ulverscroft Lane began to change into brick houses. Incomers came to outnumber old residents, particularly as the old folk died and their cottages were modernised.

Alan Brown recalls how, at school in Leicester during the thirties, and even during the war, he learnt to keep quiet about the fact that he lived in a thatched cottage in the country. Such an admission marked him out as a country yokel from a rural slum. Times change, and now his white stone and thatched cottage is seen as postcard pretty – one of the county's more idyllic houses, which only the prosperous could dream of making their own.

Post War Christmas.
Kitty Brown shares a cracker
with nephew David Snartt.

Mim's grandfather used to say of the Incomers, "I've seen them come, and I've seen them go, and I'm still here." But now he has gone, and some of the Incomers have taken root. They move around in the village, just as the natives have always done, looking for a bigger house, or a smaller. Sometimes they leave but can't settle anywhere else, so they come back.

In the years since the Second World War Newtown Linford has moved drastically up-market. Florrie Harrison grew up in an almost feudal estate village, with well water, cooking on the kitchen fire, and night-soil men on Fridays. Now from her kitchen window she overlooks a field where, from time to time, a helicopter drops in to carry off a neighbour for a day at the races.

Modest cottages (not to mention old barns) have been converted into luxurious residences, whose extensions have been extended, and whose kitchens and bathrooms have been modernised several times over. Few of the old residents live in such palaces, but they work cheerfully alongside such newcomers as wish to play an active part in village life – in the church, the W.I., the club, and so on. They don't live in the past – but they treasure their memories.